Praise for Brenda Yoho and *Lead with Two Rules: Feeling Good & Feeling Safe*

Brenda gives us a new perspective on school leadership in *Lead with Two Rules: Feeling Good & Feeling Safe*. How many of us were raised in an educational environment that followed the adage: children should be seen, but not heard. So many children go through life with personal stories of trauma, insecurities, and circumstances; the classroom (and school in general) just adds to the frustration. These children need a voice; Brenda Yoho is that voice! I appreciate how Brenda brings humanity into schools.

This is socially conscious leadership at its core. I should know—I wrote a book on it.

—Keith J. McNally, EdD. Author of *Walking the Path—A Leader's Journey* and host of the Envision Speakers Series

Brenda Yoho's book, *Lead with Two Rules: Feeling Good & Feeling Safe,* embarks on a profound journey that transcends the conventional scope of education. As someone deeply immersed in the world of teaching, training, and fostering holistic well-being through OlavatEd, I was captivated by Brenda's perspective.

As someone who passionately believes in the power of education to transform lives, I found Brenda Yoho's *Two Rules* to be a guiding light. It is a powerful resource for educators, administrators, and anyone dedicated to nurturing the holistic well-being of every learner. Brenda's book inspires us to champion inclusive and nurturing learning spaces where everyone can thrive.

Ola ElKhatib, M.Ed, Teacher, Teacher Trainer, Well-being Coach, and Founder of OlavatEd.

Brenda Yoho redefines education by prioritizing mental health over academic achievement. With a unique perspective born from personal experiences, Brenda advocates for inclusivity and the well-being of every individual. Her "Two-Rules" framework, built on genuine connections and self-compassion, offers practical strategies for educators to nurture resilience and empathy in students. This book inspires us to reshape traditional education models, recognizing the vital link between mental health and academic success.

—Noemi Beres, Co-founder of Podcast Connections

Brenda Yoho is an educator who is not only adept as a skilled, experienced practitioner, but who is equally passionate about keeping abreast of the latest in instructional and school-related pedagogy and putting the most promising of its developments into action.

As her superintendent, I respected and appreciated her dedication, instructional knowledge, willingness to try new ideas, and her big heart for students.

Her acquired knowledge about instruction and students, acquired over the decades, indeed makes for meaningful and valuable reading for any practitioner.

—Mark Denman, Superintendent Danville District 118

Lead with Two Rules: Feeling Good & Feeling Safe provides strategies and actionable plans for getting the ownership from students first and foremost, to get them to engage more deeply in their learning.

—Dr. Sharon Kherat, Ed.D,
Superintendent of Peoria Public Schools

Mentoring school leaders throughout the United States and overseas, Brenda's positive impact on the lives of our children knows no bounds. Her journey from the role of a classroom teaching assistant to classroom teacher, school principal, central office administration, and now an esteemed author and mentor for dozens of principals exemplifies her unwavering commitment to the field of education.

Brenda's problem-solving suggestions serve as a wellspring of inspiration for both young learners and seasoned educators. Her guidance transcends the boundaries of age and experience, offering valuable insights to anyone fortunate enough to learn from her. Brenda is an exemplary leader, embodying the ideals and principles that the education profession holds dear. She generously shares her real-life experiences, extensive research, and a deep-seated dedication to the betterment of education. Her wisdom and passion are the driving forces behind the transformation of countless classrooms and the future prospects of our children.

—Dianna Kirk, EdS., former Assistant Superintendent,
Danville District 118

Brenda is an energetic leader with a positive attitude, dedicated to the emotional and intellectual development of her students and staff. She makes a difference! I'm confident her book, *Lead with Two Rules: Feeling Good & Feeling Safe,* will do the same. A must read for new building administrators.

—Nanette Mellen Finkle,
former Superintendent Danville District 118

This book is easy to read with lots of examples, and ways to lessen and manage conflict while allowing kids to learn and find ways to cope along the way. What I love most is that it's a doable roadmap to making your school a safe space for students and to give them agency in the process of making it one.

—Anne Moss Rogers, MentalHealthAwarenessEducation.com,
mental health speaker and suicide education expert;
Co-author, *Emotionally Naked: A Teacher's Guide
to Preventing Suicide and Recognizing Students at Risk*

Lead with Two Rules

Feeling Good & Feeling Safe

BRENDA YOHO

ISBN 979-8-9890688-0-7 (print)
ISBN 979-8-9890688-1-4 (ebook)

Content Editor: Kate Babbitt
Production Management: Weaving Influence
Cover and Interior Design: Rachel Royer
Copyeditor: Meredith Mix
Typesetter: Lori Weidert
Proofreader: Keri Hales

Printed in the United States of America

Dedicated to Bob McMurray, who taught me to set goals to achieve;

Lynn Childs, who will always be treasured in my heart and memories;

My husband and beautiful family;

All of the families, students, communities, and staff I served.

I will always be grateful.

Contents

Foreword

In this insightful read, *Lead with Two Rules: Feeling Good and Feeling Safe,* Brenda Yoho dares to challenge the prevailing emphasis on academic achievement and invites us into a new era of education—one that prioritizes mental health. Drawing from her own personal experiences and deep commitment to inclusive education, Brenda presents a compelling case for our approach to educating young people.

Having grown up with parents who couldn't read, Brenda intimately understands the transformative power of education and the importance of creating an inclusive culture. Her work in a high-poverty, high-needs school has equipped her with firsthand knowledge of the challenges faced by students and the critical need for fostering environments that value the well-being of every individual.

At the heart of Brenda's philosophy lies the innovative "two-rules" framework, centered around authentic connection and self-compassion. These principles, inspired by her own journey, form the foundation for cultivating safe and nurturing environments within our schools. Brenda's practical strategies empower educators to foster resilience, empathy, and self-care, equipping students with essential tools for academic and emotional growth.

The Two-Rules School goes beyond theory—it is a testament to Brenda's dedication and belief in the transformative power of education. Through her personal narrative and practical guidance, she inspires me, and hopefully you, to reevaluate traditional models and embrace an approach that recognizes the intrinsic link between mental health and academic success.

Prepare to be empowered as you embark on this transformative journey. Brenda sets a path toward a future where mental health and education harmoniously intersect, nurturing compassionate and resilient individuals. Let us heed her call to action to create an inclusive and nurturing educational landscape.

Dr. Jason Leahy,
Executive Director of Illinois Principals Association

Acknowledgments of Gratitude

Thank you. Those two words are big and powerful, but at the same time, they do not reflect all an individual like me would like to express. The number of individuals in this book is so many that my memories may not allow me to capture all their names, but my heart has them stored forever. Having a traumatic brain injury, you have parts of memories that will not produce the information you need when you encounter a person from your past. However, your heart knows them, and a smile reveals the meaning and reminder of who they are to you. Everyone who has been a part of my life is reflected in the words, actions, values, and beliefs I share. As a reader, you will join this group.

This book is full of real stories from all the schools I have been involved with over my career in education. I cherish my time with all of them and the ones I continue to meet through those I coach. It is students like Diante Johnson, Rachel Adair, Natalie Weaver, Ryan Washkowiak, Kellen Williams, Elijah Williams, and all of my students who contributed to my motivation to continue to move forward with this book. The voices that echo the loudest in my heart are those whose lives were cut short by illness, self-harm, or violence. One in particular wrote the words I spoke to him often in a message to me as a gift when I left to serve at the district level, "Thank you for Never Giving Up on Me!" It is the loudest. His mother kicked him out when he turned 18, and he called me again to help him. I did, but if he only would have called me again . . . maybe he would still be alive? I don't know.

The many staff members who met with me or talked to me over the years to share their stories of our work together—Chad Turner, Meghan Siwecki, Chrissie Overley Williams, Destinia Schumann, Angelique Simmon, Jenny Slider, Tricia Keith, Robin Fluno, Wayne Able, Jessica Mullen, Jacqueline Locascio, Rose Holycross and Valarie Shelton, and many morehelped me to see the implementation of the two-rules method from their perspectives. Their contributions also helped me to see the growth within everyone as we worked as a "family" together and to understand the many different personalities, needs, and relationships involved. They understood the importance of how building a solid foundation of core values and beliefs and consistency in all we do is critical to our success.

Families, friends, and communities continue to be supportive of my efforts. Wendy R., Karrie V., Rickey W., Jeanette N,. and Janet M. are just a couple of the names to mention. The courage to trust children with others should never be forgotten, I thank the many families who have done that with me and the many staff members over the years. Sharing real feedback in wanting to grow and accepting it is an indication of wanting to lead with others in mind. Standing beside a friend in good times, sick times and in times of uncertainty is the defining feature of friendships. Communities wanting to be involved in the efforts your purpose is a signal of commitment to all in the community and in our abilities to make an impact together.

The list of leaders and key individuals who made this journey reach a point of completion for the message to be delivered in book form is quite large and wide. The span of its reach extends around the globe and into the heavens above. The leaders I can include in the list are Rev. Leon Korb, Robert Delmotte, Susan Riggle, Kevin Tate, Nanette Mellen Finkle, Dianna Kirk, Mark Denman, Dr. Sharon Desmoulin-Kherat, Dr. Jason Leahy, Dr. Sue Homes, Fred Singleton, Don Hansen, Don Dillion,

Dr. Brent Clark, Lynn Childs, Mark Neal, Gladys Davis, Alice Payne, Johnnie Carey, Val Gilbert, MaryAnn Moore, Jeanne Smith, Barb Price, and so many more. I learn from every person who has touched my path, and I am so blessed because of it. The enrichment I have received is more than I can describe in words.

Kate Babbitt, my content editor, worked with me to look deeper into why I created Two Rules, and added valuable advice as I wrote the manuscript. She worked to help me create the pages you will enjoy.

My path led me to Becky Robinson, the owner of Weaving Influence. She is an incredible individual who gives more than she hopes to ever receive. The production team at Weaving Influence is top notch. A huge thank-you goes to Rachel Royer, Lori Weidert, Meredith Mix, and Keri Hales, all of whom worked tirelessly to produce this volume you are now reading.

At times in our life journey, we may find ourselves in a place where our light is dim and fading. It is when we can find the spark from others that we can rekindle our flame. The light grows brighter as we begin to see that it only takes a spark to get a fire going again. I am so grateful to have received a spark from Weaving Influence just when I needed one, which helped me to help me begin my journey to discovering how to create a new me.

Introduction

This book tells the story of how I turned a high-poverty, high-truancy urban middle school with a poor reputation into a safe place where students felt good. High-risk students began coming to school every day because it was a place where adults they could trust cared about them and worked to help them become the best they could be.

You won't see a lot about pedagogy in this book. There are numerous books about pedagogy that focus on poverty or trauma or giving students more agency about their learning or about deeper learning, among many other topics. All of them are excellent. They are wonderful tools for educators.

This book has a different focus. It is about how principals can create a culture in their school that supports student mental health. Student mental health was rarely mentioned in the education literature until recently. Until about five years ago, if mental health was mentioned at all, it was framed as severe illness requiring hospitalization. However, today, in 2023, the young people of the United States are facing an epidemic of depression and anxiety, and the Covid pandemic has intensified this alarming trend. I know from speaking with early-career principals and colleagues who have been in the job for many years that this feels overwhelming to them. It has changed the job description for school administrators.

What I offer is a simple philosophy that is the cornerstone of a school-wide structure for monitoring student mental health and supporting students as they search for solutions to problems. It is based on two rules that students can use to make judgments about how to behave: "Will this make me (or them) feel good?" and "Will this make me (or them) feel safe?" When students master the skill of asking these two questions before they act, they learn empathy, responsibility, how to be a good friend, how to be a good community member, how to identify problems, how to identify feelings, and how to search for solutions to problems. When these two questions become the core of a school's culture, the students are creating resilience resources for themselves and for each other.

The two rules are also a promise to students from the adults in their building: We will make sure that you feel good in this school. We will make sure that you feel safe in this school. You will see stories in this book that illustrate how I supported faculty as they learned new ways of relating to students so they could keep those two promises.

A third component of the two rules is a team structure to support student mental health. Having professionals in the building who can work with students who are struggling with mental health issues accomplishes two things that make school a better place. First, teachers no longer feel that they are solely responsible for attending to the mental health needs of students in their classrooms, and second, students see that people they trust care about them and are ready to help them when they are struggling. This dynamic creates an environment that gives both students and teachers the space they need to focus on learning.

When I came to Fall Ridge Middle School, teachers were frustrated because they spent more time trying to manage their classroom than they did teaching. Some teachers felt that the students in their classrooms couldn't learn. The hallways were raucous and chaotic during class changes. Fighting was common. The truancy rate was high. For some students, school wasn't a safe place. As a result, our school had a reputation as the worst school in the district.

Within one year after I introduced the two rules, students were quiet and respectful in the hallways. Many teachers had developed caring relationships of trust with their students, and classroom management was no longer the top issue for them. Students had made several forays into the community to represent our school that had been well received. Most important of all, students understood that I and all of the other adults in their building were 100 percent on their side and were willing to do whatever it took to help them succeed.

Today, as we are in the third year of a global pandemic, every school principal in our country is coping with unprecedented levels of anxiety and depression among students at every level K–12. A job that was already hard has become immeasurably more difficult. This book is a response to the levels of stress surveys are reporting among school principals. It offers a system for creating a culture that will support them, their students, and their staff in these difficult times and those in the future.

Although the two-rules system worked in one of the toughest schools in our county, that is not to say that it turned every student around. Some weren't able to trust that the two rules would work for them, particularly when we didn't have buy-in from parents and caregivers. But on the whole, we changed a negative school culture to a nurturing one. We helped students learn emotional skills, executive skills, and behavioral skills. We created an environment that supported learning. We touched lives in ways that are still visible in our community. To this day, former students will stop me to tell me that I changed their life. Those students are now parents who are physically and emotionally present for their children in ways that their own parents weren't able to be. Students who were in situations that made them extremely high risk survived and graduated from high school. They learned new ways of coping with the levels of stress they were experiencing. The social and emotional skills they learned from applying the two rules transferred to their academic learning. We taught a generation of students how to think critically and objectively about many types of situations. Two Rules can support children K–12. All of the strategies, procedures and systems will work at every level.

This book tells you how we did it. I've written it in a conversational tone to make it easy to process when so many things are competing for your attention. In fact, you'll see quite a few actual conversations with students. Each chapter looks at one aspect of a two-rules school culture.

Chapter 1 describes how I created the two rules as a response to the hardships I saw my students enduring when I was an elementary school teacher. I felt that schools could be doing more for those students. The two rules was my way of providing more. Chapter 2 describes my experiences as I introduced the two rules at Fall Ridge. It has many suggestions for steps a principal can take as they are bringing a new approach, systems, procedures, routines and culture to their school. In chapter 3, I look at the social and emotional learning students acquire when they make the two rules part of their thought process. You'll see me using the two rules to help students understand themselves better and make plans for different choices and new behaviors. Learning the five competencies of self-awareness, self-management, social awareness, relationship skills and making decisions builds a solution-focused approach as we build resilience.

Chapter 4 focuses on supporting staff so a school keeps the promise the two rules make that everyone will feel good and everyone will feel safe. I tell stories that illustrate how I did that and how the students responded to the changes in their teachers. The chapter also looks at how a school can be a key provider of resilience resources for students. Chapter 5 discusses how a principal can support a school through trauma. It looks at working with individual students who have experienced trauma or who are living through ongoing trauma, and it provides information about how a principal can help staff and students cope with the trauma of the death of a student or staff member. Two appendices are companions to this chapter. Appendix B is a detailed description of how to plan a trauma recovery workshop for students and teachers to attend together, and Appendix C is about how a principal can provide resources that build resilience among staff.

In chapter 6, I describe the multi-tiered team structure I created at Fall Ridge that provided mental health support for students from the time they arrived on campus in the morning until they left for home in the afternoon. No student ever fell through the cracks at our school because multiple adults were monitoring each child every day. We were able to respond quickly and effectively when a student was struggling. A companion to this chapter is Appendix B, which lists all the schools in the United States that offer programs or have departments that train school psychologists. The chapter also has information about strategies principals can use to cope with the shortage of school psychologists.

The last chapter is about the mental health of school principals. We're all familiar with the idea that you can't help others unless you help yourself first. This chapter reminds principals of ways that can attend to their own mental health in the trying circumstances they face each day on the job. Appendix D, on principal mental health, discusses how to carry feelings of sadness and grief when a principal isn't able to reach a student. We all agonize over the students we couldn't help, the ones who were so damaged that they needed more than we could give them. This is a topic that isn't often discussed, and I wanted to share the place I've reached about it in the hope that it might help you.

The afterword encourages principals to make the two rules their own. What I've written in this book is a guideline. You will know what will work best in your school and how to build on the ideas I've described. The two-rules philosophy is a seed idea, something for you to expand on. I describe how I was able to expand the reach of the two rules when I became an administrator at the district level. Perhaps my story will give you some ideas about what you can ask your district to do to support the mental health of your students and staff. Two Rules can work at all grade levels.

I want to say something about the elephant in the room. How can we ethically tell children that they will be safe in our schools in an environment when school shootings are increasingly common and students participate in stressful shooter drills on a regular basis? The world students live in today is full of unprecedented dangers and stresses. I don't think anyone over the age of 35 can imagine what it's like to carry those concerns as a child.

But does that mean that we should abandon the project of providing emotional safety for kids at school? I say no. I believe we should work even harder to create an environment of trust and nurturing for students. We should build them up and provide resources for them to develop resilience skills. We should love them even harder and at the same time prepare for the worst.

Today, 95 percent of schools have active shooter drills for the whole school. Most states require them. However, a joint study by the Everytown for Gun Safety Support Fund, the American Federation of Teachers, and the National Education Association found that "there is almost no research affirming the value of active shooter drills for preventing school shootings or protecting the school community when shootings do occur." Instead, research shows that the impact of such drills on staff and students is negative and long lasting. Anxiety and depression increase significantly, and sometimes post-traumatic stress from drills lasts into adulthood. To date, there is no conclusive evidence that drills increase the safety of students and staff during a shooter event. In fact, they may give would-be shooters information they can use as they make plans.

What will decrease the chances that a school will be the target of a shooter is attending to the mental health and well-being of each student in the building. One study identified the practices schools can use that will reduce the possibility that a student will become isolated and resentful to the point that they consider becoming a shooter. These include providing strong social support and interventions when bullying occurs, ensuring that each student has a friendship network, making sure that administrators don't show favoritism in their responses to rule-breaking, and modeling respect for each student. A two-rules school does all of these things and more. The best way to prevent school shootings is to attend to the mental health needs of students every day. This book will show you how we did it at Fall Ridge. I hope you will find information here that will sustain you and give you ideas for supporting your students and staff as all of you work together toward better mental health.

1

Beginnings and Origins

Beginnings

When I was growing up, I lived in a nice house in a nice neighborhood. My family looked like a typical middle-class family in America's heartland in the 1970s: my father had a good job with GM and my mother stayed home to care for the house and the family. But we had a secret that we all worked fiercely to protect: neither of my parents could read.

Both parents came from tough backgrounds in Kentucky. As far as I know, my mother never attended school. Her father died when she was eleven. After that, she took care of the household and her younger siblings while her mother worked on the farm. Even after her mother remarried, it was Mom who did the housework and kept everything running. My father came from a family of nine. Everyone worked hard farming tobacco, hay, and corn. Dad dropped out of school after the eighth grade. He hadn't learned to read.

Dad moved the family from Kentucky to Illinois, following the pipeline to a good-paying industrial job. On the surface, everything looked okay with us. But no one knew that from the age of 10, I was writing checks for my parents, learning about banking transactions so I could accompany my father to the bank and help him, and reading important letters that came in the mail to them.

My siblings and I covered for our parents and participated in the masking they did to conceal their illiteracy. I knew instinctively how important this was, even at the age of 8. That year, my grandmother, my mother's mother, died. I was out of school for some time as the family traveled to Kentucky for the funeral. When I returned to school, I failed a test because I had missed the material in class. I had to take the test with the failing grade home and get the signature of a parent to assert that they had seen the paper.

My mother had great respect for teachers and wanted to make sure that her signature was right. She must have erased that signature at least five times because she wanted to get it right for the teacher. I was standing by her side, growing increasingly anxious as the paper looked messier and messier, wailing that it was OK; it was good enough.

I put the paper on my teacher's desk the next day. I was walking back to my seat when I heard her yell my name. I turned around to see her waving my paper in the air, yelling "*You* signed this!" Even though I shook my head no, she pointed toward the hallway and said, "Get out! I am going to call your mother!" "No, please don't call my mother," I pleaded. This seemed to make her even more angry. Everyone watched as I trudged out into the hall. The teacher didn't lower her voice when we got outside the classroom. She continued to accuse me of signing the paper myself. She just wouldn't let up. Over and over she scolded and berated me for being dishonest by forging my mother's signature. More and more people were hearing what was happening. The whole school would soon know about this event.

I never gave my mother up. As many people watched in the hallway, I said that yes, I had tried to forge her signature. I took the blame. As excruciating as the public humiliation was, it was more important to protect my mother. She couldn't ever know what had happened. Protecting her, though, meant I had no advocate who could challenge the teacher about her behavior and protect me. The teacher followed through on her threat, but when she called my home, it was my older sister who answered the phone. She came to the school and confirmed it was my mother's signature. She whispered something else to the teacher, but the teacher never apologized to me. Then my sister took me home.

School was not the same for me after that day. I learned that day what terrible injustices and harms can be done when a teacher doesn't know a student's situation. Instead of helping me in a sensitive way, she traumatized me that day. I still carry that trauma with me, and I never forgave that teacher.

Both parents worked hard to give me and my siblings a good start in life. My mother loved to make a traditional rural Sunday dinner for the family. After my older siblings married and started their own families, they would still come to our house each week for Mom's fried chicken, mashed potatoes, green beans and corn from the garden, homemade dinner rolls, and chocolate pie. My mother was never happier than when she was feeding her entire family.

She was also a talented quilter. She couldn't read patterns and had never studied mathematics, but she could see a quilt and then make it herself. Quilting involves calculation of fabric quantities, knowledge of geometry, strategizing about how to organize pieces in a pleasing design, and a great deal of planning. Without being able to write any of these details down, my mother created beautiful quilts, carrying all of the information in her head. She also made quilted hot pads and other small items to give as gifts.

But I watched her struggle. In the mid-1970s, the grocery stores in our area began using generic labels for food. Plain black lettering on a white background. No pictures. I was with her the first time she went into a store and looked down the aisle at all of those boxes and cans with only words on the labels. I saw the panic and despair and frustration on her face as she realized that she could no longer shop independently. She would need help to do the thing that gave her the greatest pleasure—making Sunday dinner for her family.

Except for their illiteracy, which is a huge exception, both parents were high-functioning, happy people. They instilled in me the value of caring for others. Every year many people from the neighborhood came to our house to receive something from the huge garden they grew. The garden was their pride and joy. No one could go into it, but they were happy to pick the produce themselves and give it to their neighbors and friends. Mom would spend hours canning or preparing corn for the freezer. She would then give food to others during the winter months. My dad helped anyone he saw in need, regardless of whether he knew them or not. He never met a person he didn't befriend.

My parents taught me to work hard, save money, and get a good education. Especially get a good education. I was the first person in my family to graduate from college. But one degree wasn't enough for me; after my BA, I earned an MA in education. I became a teacher.

Two incidents from my childhood had a lasting impact on who I became. When I was in kindergarten, I made a friend. Tammy helped me with the buttons on my coat because they were hard for me to do. We did everything together at school: we walked each other to the restroom; we sat together in the library; we played together at recess. Tammy made me feel good and safe at school. She was Black, but I didn't know that was supposed to be an issue. I went home and told my parents that I wanted Tammy to come to our house for a playdate. My dad listened carefully and thought for a moment, then he slowly said, "I don't think that would be a good choice for Tammy's family." I was very perplexed. I couldn't imagine what my friendly father, who liked every-one he met, meant by those words.

As I got older, I began to realize that he had been trying to protect my friend. He knew that many people in the neighborhoods around us were virulently racist and that a Black girl entering a white household to play with a little white girl on an equal basis might trigger a serious response from the community. He was trying to protect my friend and I guess probably us as well.

The second incident happened when I was in the fifth grade. We had a Black male schoolteacher that year. It was the first time a Black teacher had been hired in our district. The community reacted to his presence with actions designed to intimidate him. Several girls in my grade level made allegations to their families about his behavior. They had stated several times about how he wanted them to wear dresses, I can recall. I was not in the classroom or had any interactions with him. I knew some of the girls. In response to these allegations, members of the KKK burned a cross on his lawn. I had never seen anything like this before and it made me afraid. We saw a willingness to threaten and do harm in our middle-class neighborhood in the heartland in the 1970s. One day our teacher was gone and I never knew why.

As I entered the teaching profession, I had lots of preparation in the school of life. I knew that a family's façade could mask a serious problem. I knew that a serious problem wasn't the only story a family has to tell. I knew what it felt like to lack an advocate because of a parent's deficit. I knew that helping others was important. I knew that a community could be a force for good and a force for evil. I learned that some people judged others according to the color of their skin. And I knew that teachers could harm or help depending on how they interacted with students.

The Origins of the Two-Rules Framework

I began my career in education as a teaching assistant. At the time I had an associate's degree. During the six years I did that job, I attended school part-time and earned a BA. I was the first person in my family to get a college degree. I gradually worked my way up the ladder in schools in the county where I had grown up. I taught reading, math, and computer skills to kindergarteners through fifth graders for four years, then I was a fifth-grade classroom teacher for two years. After I had taught for two years, I began working toward an advanced degree. When I earned my MA in education, I became an assistant principal and then a principal at a middle school that had a reputation for many problems with gangs and drugs. Although the county where I worked in education for twenty years was largely rural, our schools in the county's small city had many of the problems that urban schools were facing.

There was a reason for that. By the 1990s and early 2000s, the economy of the county had changed. The days were gone when a father could support a family with a factory job and a mother could stay home to run the household, as my parents had done in the 1970s and 1980s. Many factories closed down. The biggest hit came in 1996, when General Motors closed down its factory and sent those jobs overseas. GM had employed 3,000 people at one time and the loss hit our county hard. In many households, both parents needed to work. The jobs that were available paid lower and had fewer benefits than the industrial jobs the county had lost. Some people worked two or even three jobs. Sometimes one parent would work second shift and the other would work third shift.

The effects of the economic downturn showed up in schools in many ways. As many as one in four of the students in the schools where I worked were classified as at risk. In my student teaching year, more than 50 percent of the students in my classroom were in households at the poverty level or that were considered low income. Some adults turned to drugs and alcohol as a way of coping with economic stress, with the result that one parent was absent in many homes. Some pre-adolescent kids were shopping and preparing meals for younger siblings. Some kids had access to drugs. Some already had mental health issues. Many were struggling to acquire basic skills in reading and math. Some students carried such heavy burdens from their home life that they were shut down. They were so withdrawn at school that it seemed impossible to reach them. And some kids just didn't show up. Truancy was a significant problem in our district.

I felt great empathy for my students. I knew that they needed school to be a place where they could set their burdens aside for eight hours a day. They needed school to be a place where they felt welcome and valued. They needed to *feel right* in order to learn.

It wasn't popular in the 1990s and early 2000s to think about the emotional well-being of students as a key component of education. Or of any job, really. When I was in high school, an adult had told me that I wasn't a good fit for the field of social work because I was too emotional. But I knew that emotions were important. And I vividly remembered the traumatic experience of having my third-grade teacher humiliate me about the signature on my test paper. For years after that, I experienced school as a place where I wasn't safe.

I realized that the education system I was working in wasn't meeting the needs of many students. Some teachers paid attention to students who learned easily and ignored students who were struggling. They wanted to teach students who wouldn't challenge them and they didn't want to battle with those who would cause problems. I was now in a position to see school through the lens of an educator, but I wondered what school looked like to the struggling students. What did they see? What did they feel? What did they need? What did they want?

Making Choices and Asking Questions

The process I was going through as an educator became a key component of the two-rules framework. I was asking questions when I saw a need. And I continued to ask questions until I reached a good answer. A questioning mindset became the bedrock of the philosophy I was developing.

Another thing I noticed was that kids were trying to solve issues without the problem-solving skills they needed. One boy came to school with a wet coat one day. His coat had become very dirty and he had washed it himself, but he didn't realize that he needed to factor in drying time and he didn't know how long a winter coat would need in the dryer. Like many students in our county, he was dealing with issues that children aren't supposed to deal with. Children are supposed to have homes where adults provide food and clothing and warmth. But many kids in our district didn't have that. What could I do to help them cope with the situations they faced?

I saw children who were so overwhelmed that they couldn't cope at all. One little boy would get so overwhelmed that he would run out of the school and hide under a bush. He needed a safe place while he regained control of his feelings and hiding under a bush was the best solution he could think of.

I began to think about teaching students how to think through potential scenarios of actions they might take in response to the problems they were facing. One key idea emerged from a computer lab I ran for fifth graders. When you operate a computer, each keystroke has a definite consequence every time. When you use different keystrokes, there are different consequences. I asked my students what were all the possible ways they could use computers to get the results they wanted. Were there other paths to their goal? Then I helped them transfer that cognitive skill to other areas of their lives.

In my lab, we used a software program written by Tom Snyder titled "Decisions, Decisions," an early role-playing video game that asked students to collectively analyze a problem from many points of view and make a decision about how to address the problem. Students would enter their solution into a computer and see what outcome that decision led to. Titles in this series put students in the roles of environmental activists, a family managing its household budget, or an advisor to a political candidate. This software was very popular with fifth graders, and while they had a good time working through the software, they were also learning about seeing issues from the perspective of someone who was different from them. The software programs I used in my computer lab focused not only on the content of the curriculum but also on the importance of choices, decisions, and innovation in making life better for others. That was the spark that got me thinking about all of the choices we make and how those choices impact what we do, who we are, and how we live our lives.

The Importance of Safety

I realized that physical safety was also a big issue for many kids in our district. Using the questioning pedagogy I was developing, I began working with students who spent time alone at home to help them figure out what they needed. I would ask them: "Do you feel safe at home? What do you need to do to feel safe? What are things you can do when you don't feel safe?" These sessions helped students form proactive plans that would guide their decisions and actions. I couldn't fix the structural problems that put kids in difficult situations, but I could help them develop the questioning mindset that would enable them to cope.

During my years as a teaching assistant and a teacher, I was hired with federal Title I funds. The name of this program changed over the years; you're probably more familiar with the No Child Left Behind program (2002–2015) or the Every Student Succeeds Act (2016–present). These programs target low-income students who are at risk academically. Because I was hired with these funds, I was able to develop programs to support at-risk students as part of my job.

I always made emotional well-being part of my work with at-risk kids. I worked with small groups of students and often formed relationships of mutual trust with them. Shut-down kids would eventually trust me enough to tell me why they were so sad. That gave me opportunities to create situations where they could succeed. I was determined to break down the obstacles that prevented at-risk students from seeing what they could be. I wanted each of them to know that someone wanted them to do well.

Over the years as I worked with students to help them cope with their situations at home and at school, I found myself asking them the same questions over and over again. And all of my questions related to two main issues: feeling good and feeling safe. All of the rules in the student handbook were about one or the other of those two things. The problems our students were facing were serious. Every student in our schools, regardless of their situation at home, was contending with large problems that would challenge any adult. They needed skills for navigating their way through their difficulties so they could reach a successful adulthood.

By the time I became the principal of a middle school, I was talking openly with students about problems. That was the framework I was using. I told them that they could be part of the problem or part of the solution. I asked them which they wanted to be. Of course they all wanted to be part of the solution. "All right," I would say. "Good. Here are two rules that will make you a problem solver. Two questions to ask yourself: 'Will I feel good if I do this? Will I feel safe if I do this?'" I was ready to lead a two-rules school.

2

Creating a Two-Rules Culture in a Middle School

Humans are to be respected at all times.
—Eva Kor

The Two Rules philosophy is a promise to students that their welfare is the center of a school's culture: Everyone will feel good in this school, and everyone will feel safe in this school. It is also a request that students work to ensure that both of these statements are true every day. In Chapter 3, you will see the Two Rules philosophy in action as I worked with students who came to me for discipline. This chapter is about the promise to students and how I communicated it.

The Social Context of Fall Ridge Middle School

When I became the principal of Fall Ridge in 2008, I had been working in education in the county I grew up in for eighteen years: six years as a teaching assistant, seven years as a teacher, and five years in administration. During those years, I had gradually developed a system for interacting with students that put their well-being and their needs first. My system was based on relationships and mutual respect. For example,

I had learned that silently signaling to a classroom that I wanted quiet with a raised hand was more effective than raising my voice and yelling. Students responded to this because they knew I was on their side and respected them.

I knew my community well and I knew it was in crisis. The contrast between the childhoods the students in my school were having and my own childhood could not have been more stark. I was raised in a two-parent home that was supported by the income of one parent. In my county, even a high school dropout could get a good-paying job at GM and support a family when I was growing up. My parents were very involved in my education and made it clear that college was in my future. I was surrounded by a close-knit community of adults who cheered each accomplishment I achieved.

Few of the students in the classrooms of my school had that kind of support. In the small midwestern city where the school was located, over 40 percent of the households were headed by women with children. Many parents of our students worked two or even three jobs and still struggled to make ends meet. During the years I was an administrator at that school, between 80 and 90 percent of the students were categorized as low income—that is, children whose families qualified for the Supplemental Nutrition Assistance Program, were in foster care, or qualified for reduced-price or free school lunches.

In our city, the high school dropout rate was 40 percent higher than the national rate. Only 6.4 percent of the adults in the city had a bachelor's degree or higher. There weren't any large companies with good-paying jobs to hire dropouts in our county anymore. When these students looked at the lives of the adults they knew, what they saw was economic insecurity, very little postsecondary education, and hard work for low pay.

In addition, the racial composition of our county had changed since my childhood. In the 1990s, public housing in a major city near us was torn down to make way for better-quality housing. City officials advised many displaced Black families to move to nearby counties. Over the years of my tenure as principal of a middle school, the percentage of

Black students hovered around 40 percent in a state where the Black population overall was around 20 percent. The families of these students struggled with issues that people who had been born in the county didn't face, including coping with the trauma of displacement, dealing with the culture shock of moving to a largely rural environment, entering an economy with few job opportunities, and adjusting to an environment in which the majority was a different race.

During the years when I was at this school, the Black incarceration rate across the country was increasing rapidly. In 2000, the Black population of our state was just over 15 percent, but Black men and women accounted for 49 percent of the prison population. By 2010, that number had climbed to 57.8 percent and the vast majority of Black prisoners in our state were men. As a result, the proportion of Black households with children headed by women in our city was much larger than the proportion of white households in that category.

Research on School Climate in 2008

Researchers were tentative about the issue of school climate in the 2010s. After several decades of a strong focus on academic achievement, many educators and researchers saw an emotionally nurturing, positive school climate as the soft side of the middle school mission, something that distracted from the primary goal of high-enough grades and scores. When I converted a junior high school to a two-rules middle school as an assistant principal in the early 2000s, I got a lot of pushback from the teachers; they felt that I was trying to make their junior high school more like an elementary school with my focus on emotions. For many middle school educators, "developmentally appropriate," the starting place of the middle school mission in the 1960s and the phrase that was included in every article or book about that mission, meant cognitive development, not emotional development.

Research in the 1990s and early 2000s had begun to report on the links between emotional state and ability to learn, though. In the mid-1990s, epidemiologists estimated that 12 to 30 percent of school-age children in the United States were experiencing "at least moderate behavioral, social, or emotional problems."[1] Researchers had begun to show a strong link between depression and poor academic performance.[2] One longitudinal study found that signs of emotional distress in seventh grade were associated with lower grades by the end of the eighth-grade year.[3] Several studies found that "conduct problems are associated with poor academic performance."[4] Researchers found that students with behavioral problems were likely to be put on lower academic tracks, especially Black students.[5] A handful of studies found that behavioral problems "predict subsequent problem behaviors, such as delinquency, drug abuse, and dropping out of school."[6]

All of these studies had instrumentalist agendas: attend to the emotional needs of students so they can get better grades and avoid the common pitfalls of at-risk students. I was certainly interested in the academic achievements of our students, but my primary focus was the welfare of our students as human beings. At Fall Ridge, at least 75 percent of our students were struggling with emotional and mental health issues that manifested in their behavior at school. Most were trying to cope with survival issues every day: Would there be a drive-by shooting in their neighborhood today? How could they get food after school that day? How could they avoid getting sick in the winter when they didn't own a warm winter coat? Could they avoid an angry alcoholic parent after school? Could they protect themselves from sexual abuse at night?

One of my primary goals as the principal of Fall Ridge was making sure students' primary physical and emotional needs were attended to. I knew they wouldn't be able to focus on learning until those things happened. That was why I brought a nurturing leadership style to the school that was unfamiliar and even startling to some students and faculty. I wanted every student to feel good and feel safe for every moment they were on our school campus.

Two Rules for the School

I knew that my system was new for teachers and for many students. My first task was to establish trust with them. On the first day of school, I called a school-wide assembly. Over 600 students and their teachers crowded into the gymnasium. The first thing I did was ask all the teachers to leave. Everyone looked at me like I was a crazy person. No one had ever done something like that before. None of the teachers moved. I said, "Seriously, staff, just take ten minutes and go get a snack or take a restroom break. Then you can come back." After a few long seconds, a few teachers stood up and began to move toward the door. One teacher stopped near me and said, "Are you sure you want to do this?" This was a school with a reputation for having frequent fights, unruly classroom behavior, and boisterous behavior on buses. The teachers were worried that I would lose control of a gymnasium full of 600 students. "Absolutely," I answered.

Finally all the teachers had left the room, but I could see them standing in the hallway. I said to the students, "They are standing in the hallway. They're peeking in the windows. They don't trust me yet. They don't know me yet." The students laughed. "But they will get to know me, just like you and I will get to know each other." I wanted to convey to them that I was interested in real relationships with each of them, that each of them would be much more than just a name to me.

The previous year, my predecessor had used the first day of school to talk about test scores. He emphasized that students needed to work harder to get their scores up so the school wouldn't lose federal money. That was not my message to the students of Fall Ridge. I told them that it was a privilege for me to be working at their school. I said that I had heard that the reputation of their school was that it was the worst school in the city and that I rejected that view completely. "We want only the best for our school. I hope you will help me make sure that everyone who walks through our doors knows this and everyone in our community knows this."

I went on to introduce the two rules. "I have only two rules, so it should be pretty easy to learn them. Rule one: Everyone who walks through the doors of this school is going to feel good about being here. Rule two: Everyone who walks through the doors of this school is going to feel safe while they are here. So it sounds pretty easy. Here's how you can help follow those rules. Before you say or do something, ask yourself these questions: 'Is this going to make me feel good? Is this going to make me feel safe? Is this going to make others feel good? Is this going to make others feel safe?' If the answer to any of those questions is no, then you shouldn't do it. If you do it, you are choosing to be part of the problem."

I told the students what soon became my mantra: "You can choose to be part of the problem or part of the solution. The choice is yours to make." I introduced the idea that being part of the problem was a choice that already had solutions. Those solutions were in the rules handbook for the school, which outlined all the consequences for problematic behavior. "But," I told them, "you will not need that handbook if you follow the two rules and ask the questions." I also introduced the idea that we would work together on being responsive rather than reactive. I closed by saying, "If you have a problem, we have lots of resources to help you. My door is always open."

In this short speech, I introduced the entire two rules framework and let students know that I wanted to be their partner in finding solutions to the school's problems and to their own individual problems. I let them know that their well-being was my top priority. This approach was very surprising to the students. This was a district where, as a social worker at the Center for Children's Services, a local agency, later said, "Often principals or teachers had little positive to say and the kids knew it." Students stopped by me on their way out of the gym to tell me that they liked what I had said and they liked my approach to them. I had laid the groundwork for the most important element of a two-rules school: relationships of trust and caring between the principal and the students.

I kept my promise about my open door. Students soon learned that if they had the courage to come see me in my office with a problem, I would drop everything to talk with them. My secretary knew that when a student wanted to see me, she was to interrupt a meeting if necessary so I could come out and talk with them. Students sometimes came to my office first thing in the morning when there was trouble brewing for them and they needed my help to find a solution. They soon became very comfortable approaching me when they needed help. In this way, I was able to work with students to prevent fights. Parents and caregivers also knew that I was ready to be available to them any time they called or came to the school. I was there to help them find solutions to their challenges.

I will say more about how faculty were involved with the two rules in later chapters. For now, I will say that I focused on winning their trust. I did not insist that they follow the two rules in their classrooms; I did not want to impose my ideas in a heavy-handed way. The two rules was a system that I chose to use in my interactions with students and in my work to establish a positive culture in our school.

I used the same approach with faculty that I did with students. I focused on listening to what they told me and understanding where they were at the moment. I knew that all of us were facing our own difficulties, challenges, and obstacles. I wanted to hear from them what they needed. I told them that I would be transparent and honest with them and that I would roll up my sleeves to work alongside them to solve the issues in our school. I also told them that accepting the status quo for the school was a choice and that we did not need to accept mediocrity. I told them that they could provide hope for students by showing them that they believed in them and wanted the best for them.

Although faculty had the autonomy to choose to participate or not, many of them became enthusiastic adopters of the two-rules approach when they saw the changes in student behavior as their relationships with me developed. This was the case even for those who had been teaching for many years and had stopped believing that the students in our school could be helped. The word that pops up often in teachers' memories of my years at Fall Ridge is "family." The students, the teachers, and I became a family characterized by warm, caring relationships of trust.

Communicating the Two-Rules Philosophy to Students

Respect for Students Is Key

I learned a lesson about respect from my good friend Eva Kor, who was a Holocaust survivor. She and her sister had survived Dr. Josef Mengele's horrifying experiments with twins during the Holocaust. I knew her during my teaching years and spent many hours with her. Eva wanted people to know about this tragic episode in history and built a Holocaust museum and learning center in her city. Late in life, she received a letter that invited her to Washington, DC, to meet with one of the men who had held her prisoner. At first she said she wouldn't go, but in the end she went because she didn't want to hold on to her pain anymore. She chose to forgive.

After that, Eva became a forgiveness advocate. She said that forgiveness was for the benefit of the survivor, not the perpetrator. She taught that forgiveness doesn't condone evil deeds and doesn't preclude seeking justice. Her main point was that forgiveness brings peace to the survivor and prevents future violence. She wrote, "We can teach people that when they are hurting, instead of acting out of pain they can heal themselves through forgiveness."[7]

When I asked her to come to my school to tell her story so my students could learn about tolerance, she vehemently rejected my request. I was puzzled by this response and asked her why. I thought she could explain the concept of tolerance to the kids perfectly. She responded, "No, you should not be teaching this word to them. You tolerate a mosquito buzzing in your ear, you do not tolerate humans. Humans are to be respected at all times." I was schooled that day and I never forgot the lesson she taught me.

During the years I was putting the pieces of the two-rules system together, I built respect for students into every aspect of my work. No matter where a student is, they deserve respect. That includes students in the middle of a meltdown, students who can't control their anger, students who have just created a problem in the classroom, students who have checked out emotionally and aren't engaging with anyone. All of them are human beings in struggle who have the right to respectful interactions from the adults they see at school.

This also applies to parents. In my work with families in my district, I encountered parents who were neglecting or harming their children, parents who were in trouble with the law, parents who couldn't meet basic needs of their children, parents who were engaging in risky behavior. No matter where they were, I gave them respect. I always remembered that where they were at the time was not the end of their story. Like their children, they had the power to make choices that could move them to a different place. An interaction with a judgmental school principal would not help them, but respectful support maybe could. When I talked with parents, I always let them know that I considered being responsible for the welfare of their children a privilege. I would say, "Thank you for trusting me with your child for eight hours a day."

Students, families, and caregivers reciprocated the trust I showed them. I told students that when I wanted to talk with them, I would hold up my hand. I asked them to hold their hands up in response. This was a respectful and effective way to gain the attention of a group of students. One night I attended a sporting event at our high school gymnasium. Students and families from two middle schools were present to watch the staff and students play basketball together. During the event, a fight broke out in the stands. It was a delicate moment that could have turned dangerous very quickly. The gym was crowded and many people were yelling. I walked to the center of the gym and raised my hand. Students responded immediately by raising their hands too. The adults saw what the kids were doing and also raised their hands. Within five minutes the gym was completely quiet and order was restored. That is what mutual respect can do for a school.

Daily Communication of Two Rules to Students

Changing the culture of a school was a process. It was about building places, tools, resources, and opportunities to teach my message in every place I could. One of the first things I did was buy a full-length mirror and mount it horizontally on the bulletin board in the main hallway of the school. This reminded students to reflect about the issues they faced. I would change the message above the mirror periodically with questions. The very first one was "Are you part of the problem or part of the solution today?" Other messages said, "How can we do better?" or "What do you see reflected in the mirror today? We see leaders!" or "If the reflection is not what you want, make a change." or "Do you have a problem? See someone, we have solutions!"

Slowly we began to see change ripple through the school. The question "Do you want to be part of the problem or part of the solution?" gained a solid hold in the culture of the school. The idea that they could be problem solvers appealed to our students. One of the first signs of change was hallway behavior. Our passing periods took students past classrooms still in session and it was important to not disrupt this time. So safe hallways (no pushing, shoving, running, or yelling) and feeling good about learning was our first goal. Students began walking quietly in single file past classrooms and offices. This change happened quite soon. It was a validation of my approach. My predecessor had used a military style of discipline in the hallways with limited success. Asking students to change their behavior as a way to contribute to improving their community was more effective.

Another sign of change was the decrease in the number of fights. In Chapter 3, you will see some scripts for working with students both before and after fights happen. Fighting violated both of the two rules: they didn't make students feel good or safe. Students who fought realized that they were part of the problem. This was powerful motivation for them to work on changing that behavior. All of the students at Fall Ridge wanted to be part of the solution. The idea that they had the ability to change their school environment was empowering for them.

But the biggest impact for me was the smiles I began to see on students' faces, the eye contact students began to make with me, and the trust that was building each day. The students and I had begun a partnership based on mutual respect that had great potential for learning and change.

Principal Visibility: Your Strongest Asset

Your best, most effective asset for communicating the two rules to students is yourself. Allocate time every day to be in the hallways with students—and not with the primary goal of monitoring their behavior. The primary goal of hallway time is to connect with students, to say hello, to say a word of praise, to let them know that they are valued members of your school community. Spend your lunch hour with them in the cafeteria. Talk with them about their school projects. Learn the composition of their friendship networks and make sure every student has one. Make it clear that you are there to have positive interactions with them and that you are their ally. Say their name when you speak to them—that one thing means more to students than you may realize. Thank them at every opportunity for the work they are doing to help everyone feel good and feel safe. When you see a student intervening in a verbal bullying situation, thank them for their actions to make their school a safe place. When you see two students working through a conflict, thank them for choosing to work hard to help each other feel good. When you notice that a student has modified their hallway behavior, thank them for working to keep everyone safe during passing times.

Make it clear to each student that their safety is important to you and that you want to make sure they feel good while they are at school. These ideas may surprise students at first. They may be used to hearing that rules are rules and that breaking them means consequences that separate them from their friends through detention, suspension, or even expulsion. The list of rules in the handbook may seem daunting to them and they may be worried that they won't be able to follow all of them. But when all of those rules are slotted into two categories that are clearly about their well-being and they learn a simple tool that will help them follow all school policies, their attitude toward rules may change. They may become invested in working to follow them.

You may be skeptical about my claim that all handbook policies fall into two categories related to emotional well-being and safety. Figure 2.1 is a sample of handbook policies from five middle schools in different regions of the country.

One of the most surprising ways I conveyed my concern for student safety was riding the bus. When a driver reported unsafe bus behavior, I would be on that bus the very next morning. The students' eyes would practically pop out of their heads when they saw me sitting behind the driver when they boarded the bus. They would ask why I was there and I would say, "I am here because I'm concerned about your safety. I want every student on this bus to know they are safe. I need to make sure that that is the case." Then I would follow up the next day to make sure my message had gotten across. I rarely had to ride the same bus twice. My approach wasn't punitive; I wasn't there to catch students misbehaving so I could refer them to the dean of students for punishment. I was there to make sure that they were safe. For students whose safety at home and in their neighborhoods was fragile, that was a powerful message. It may have been the first time some of them heard those words from a caring adult.

I didn't spend a lot of time in my office during the school day. (You can see more about how I allocated my time in Chapter 7.) I prioritized spending time with students so I could get to know them better. The more I could learn about each student—what their friendship network was, who they ate lunch with, what their home situation was like, what their interests were—the better I was able to build a strong relationship with them.

Figure 2.1. *Middle school policies are about feeling good and feeling safe*

Policy Category	Feel Good	Feel Safe
Rules about interactions with other students (e.g., prohibiting bullying, fighting, use of racial slurs, gang signs, physical and verbal assaults)	X	X
Drugs and alcohol (e.g., no sales of drugs or alcohol on school property; no use of tobacco, alcohol, or drugs on the bus)	X	X
Attendance (e.g., prohibiting unauthorized absence from school campus during the school day, requiring a note from a parent or caregiver when absent)	X	X
Behavior at school (e.g., prohibiting insubordination or verbal threats to staff, prohibiting bookbags or backpacks in class, prohibiting earbuds when walking in hallway)	X	X
Personal and school property (e.g., prohibiting setting off fire alarms, stealing, destroying other people's property, bringing weapons to school grounds, making bomb threats)	X	X
Dress code (e.g., prohibiting gang paraphernalia)		
Riding the bus (e.g., requiring students to behave in a quiet, orderly way at bus stops; prohibiting throwing things while on the bus)		
Other (e.g., not allowing visitors to enter the building without photo ID, requiring parents to pick up students within 15 minutes after extracurricular activities end)	X	X

We made some changes in how students got off the bus and entered the school. This was so we could greet each student, say something positive to them, and get a quick read on their body language and demeanor. Instead of students getting off all the buses at once and entering the building in one of two doors, we worked with the drivers with radio communication so that only three buses were emptied at one time. I was there to greet each student, as was the assistant principal, the dean of students, and teachers who were on a rotation for this duty. Students could enter the building through only one door instead of choosing one of two. Inside the door, a teacher was waiting to greet them. Our school resource officer was in the area to say good morning. In the back of the school, another teacher was ready to greet students. All of us had radios so we could communicate with each other. We all made a point to greet each student by name, tell them we were glad to see them, and say something positive to them. We wanted to make sure that each student had a good start to their day. Each student at Fall Ridge was welcomed and acknowledged by name as an important member of our school community by a group of adults every day.

In the lunchroom, I would talk to groups of friends about how I had noticed that they were working together to make improvements and remind them that they had the power to make good choices. I talked constantly about remembering to reflect on the two rules before they took an action. I reminded students every day that they had the power to find solutions to their problems and that I and many staff members were there to help them with that process.

We used visual information to acknowledge students' work to support the two rules. A poster in the hallway might have a photo of a student holding the door for another student using a walker. The caption would say, "Taking turns. It's all about being safe." A photo of students talking with our school resource officer would be captioned, "Together we can solve problems before they start." One of our teachers worked with students who created a model webpage about social media safety. It had messages about protecting your identity online by not sharing details that would give someone your location and about not trusting people you don't know who approach you online. The page wasn't posted to the web, but we made it accessible to all the students through our shared server. Any time we saw students doing work to contribute to our two-rules culture, we celebrated it.

Personalizing Discipline

When I worked with students using the two-rules philosophy, my goal was to help them understand their feelings and the motives for the actions that landed them in my office for discipline. (You can see more about this in Chapters 3 and 4.) I helped them learn to ask question after question that took them to deeper levels of self-awareness and empowered them to identify practical steps toward moving forward in a healthier way. This was hard work for students and it asked a lot of them.

I always followed up with these students. If we agreed that a student would try a new behavior for two weeks, I would check with them in two weeks to see how it was going. If the student was still struggling, we would work together to figure out how to tweak their plan so it led to success. Sometimes students would follow up with me before those two weeks were up. Many times, a student approached me during lunchtime, beaming with pride, to tell me that they were succeeding with their new behavior. In those moments, I always reinforced the two-rules principle that they had used their power to make a good choice and thanked them for being part of the solution.

Periodically, I would send postcards to the homes of students to thank them for the work they were doing to contribute to our two-rules school. I always used specific examples of things that student had done. A personalized postcard from the principal goes a long way toward giving students confidence about your sincerity when you say you care about them.

Collaborative Goal Setting

Once a month, I would put a large poster in the hallway of each grade-level area that had two columns. The first column showed data about where that grade had begun with a particular issue related to discipline, academics, or attendance and where they were currently with that issue. The data would come from the team leaders for that grade. Also in that first column would be several ideas that would contribute to further improvement. The second column was left blank so students could add Post-It Notes about their ideas or comments about the issue the poster focused on. We also asked them to post notes about the issues they would like to work on the next month.

The next month's poster would focus on an issue the students had identified. Teams would work with students on that issue and help them problem-solve when they were struggling. This was done at the group level and with individual students who needed extra help. The entire grade was thus working together on a focused goal that students chose each month.

Feedback from the Community

Each month we had an all-school assembly to review safety rules and the procedure for lockdown drills. I also reviewed with the students how they were doing with hallway behavior, classroom behavior, conduct at sporting events, and conduct in the community. I had told students on my first day that we would make sure our school had the best reputation in the community instead of the worst, and these assemblies reminded students how they could work to make that happen.

The monthly assemblies were a time to celebrate the positive changes in our school's culture and reputation. Within a few months, it wasn't that unusual for a cashier in the grocery store to say to me, "Mrs. Yoho, we had some students from Fall Ridge in here the other day. Their behavior was so respectful. I was so impressed!" We did several projects that took students into the community so they could see how much their neighbors and other community members valued them. On one occasion, students made slips of paper with positive messages and took them to a grocery store, where they volunteered as baggers. Each customer got one of those slips with a message to encourage them or make them smile. Another time, students made bookmarks with positive messages on them. They distributed them to local libraries and the libraries of elementary schools. Students decorated placemats for a local restaurant and signed them with their name and the name of their school. Patrons at that restaurant were reminded that Fall Ridge students were doing good work in the community.

I worked with students and coaches about behavior at sporting events. I told coaches that I wouldn't tolerate unsportsmanlike behavior at any games or practices. Any student who behaved that way would be sent to the locker room for the rest of the game. I told students who attended games how to represent our school in the best possible way and they responded. Fall Ridge students were known for their respectful demeanor at sporting events, even when their team lost.

The reputation of the school began to change as parents, caregivers, and community members saw these behaviors. I began to hear from people from many walks of life how impressed they were with Fall Ridge students. I made sure to pass those messages to students during our monthly assemblies. I had told them they had the power to change our school's culture and I wanted to make sure they understood that it was their positive choices that were making that happen. Students soon began to be proud of their school and the community they had created together.

Program Example:
Drop Everything and Read Day

A significant number of Fall Ridge students had reading test scores that were very close to meeting state standards. A second group had scores that were close to exceeding those standards. Instead of separating those students from the rest of the school in a special group that took time away from electives or after-school activities, I took an all-school approach to helping these students improve their skill level.

As part of that effort, each year we had an all-school, all-day event called Drop Everything and Read. Everyone read the same book for an entire day at school. When I proposed this meeting to our Building Leadership Team,[1] they were very skeptical. They said things like "These students don't like to read and I know for sure they're not going to stay with reading for a whole day" and "This just isn't going to work." But I persisted and convinced them to work with me to prepare for it.

I asked those team members to select a book we would read that first year that was related to how students could focus on two rules. They chose Paul Langan's *The Bully* (Townsend Press, 2002). The Building Leadership Team members created classroom materials teachers could use as the basis for follow-up activities, discussions, and writing prompts. They also coordinated a guest speaker who would introduce the book to students in an all-school assembly at the beginning of Drop Everything and Read Day. Every student got a copy of the book at the assembly and followed along as the guest speaker read the first chapter to them. Then students went to their homerooms and various community members came in to read chapters to students. (I used electives teachers to provide contractual relief periods to the homeroom teachers.)

Our guest readers included the mayor, members of the city council, members of the school board, the chief of police, police officers, members of the fire department, members of the local Black Caucus, the district superintendent, the assistant superintendent of schools, the building and grounds director (who was also a bishop in a local church), the director of the Boys and Girls Club, and the director of Big Brothers/Big Sisters. The students were astonished and pleased that all of these prominent community members came to their school to help them with their reading.

At the end of the day, the book wasn't finished and the students couldn't wait to get home so they could continue reading. They talked about the book so enthusiastically that some of the parents read it too.

We stayed with the bullying theme for two more years. The second year we read Sharon G. Flake's *Begging for Change* (Jump at the Sun, 2003), and the third year we used *We Beat the Street: How a Friendship Pact Led to Success,* by Sampson Davis, George Jenkins, and Rameck Hunt (Puffin Books, 2005). *The Bully* was about a male bully, *Begging for Change* was about a female bully, and *We Beat the Street* was about group bullying. So a generation of sixth, seventh, and eighth graders learned about the dynamics of and remedies for bullying from a variety of perspectives. That gave us a rich knowledge base to draw from when bullying issues arose at Fall Ridge. Because we knew that this topic might trigger memories or responses to trauma from students, we alerted the school social worker, the school psychologist, and the team leaders to be ready in case students approached them for help with bullying after this event.

We also alerted the local media about Drop Everything and Read. Students were amazed to see that a reporter was interested in what they were doing and even more surprised to see coverage of their event in the newspaper. These were kids who felt invisible and ignored in their hometown. Seeing so much attention from city leaders gave them a new perspective on their relationship to their community.

The first year, we used federal grant money to pay for the books, but in subsequent years a local foundation helped pay for them. That was more evidence for students that their community cared about their learning.

This annual event accomplished multiple goals:

- Students learned that prominent community members were interested in their learning.

- Students who needed extra support for reading got help without being singled out or labeled.

- Students had a positive reading experience that whetted their appetite to read more.

- The whole school learned about bullying in a positive environment.

- Students read about people their age working to find a solution to a problem they could relate to.

- Subsequent classroom activities were related to something students had enjoyed together.

- Each student owned at least one book after this event.

You can read about the function and responsibilities of the Building Leadership Team at Fall Ridge in Chapter 6.

Resource List

Ken Blanchard and Randy Conley, *Simple Truths of Leadership: 52 Ways to Be a Servant Leader and Build Trust* (Berrett-Koehler, 2022).

Ken Blanchard has been training leaders since 1979. Simple Truths of Leadership is a distillation of what he has learned about servant leadership, which he defines as leadership that provides vision while "working side by side in relationship with your people" in ways that help them accomplish agreed-upon goals. Randy Conley has translated Ken's knowledge into "simple, actionable principles that help people experience more authentic and fulfilling relationships." Blanchard wrote the first section on servant leadership and Conley wrote the second section on building trust. Throughout the book, readers will find concrete suggestions about how to put Blanchard and Conley's principles into action.

Anthony Muhammad, *Transforming School Culture: How to Overcome Staff Division,* 2nd ed. (Solution Tree, 2009).

This edition provides a school improvement plan for leaders seeking to create a positive school culture while improving relationships with staff and meeting the needs of skeptical or disillusioned staff. Chapter 1 explores reforming school culture to serve students from all racial and economic groups. Chapter 2 looks at how to overcome the tensions between building a positive, equitable school culture and meeting accountability demands. The next four chapters divide faculty into four groups based on their responses to school culture reform (the believers, the tweeners, the survivors, and the fundamentalists). The last two chapters delve into strategies for dealing with faculty pushback and introducing reform in ways that will bring in all faculty groups.

Anthony Muhammad and Luis Cruz, *Time for Change: Four Essential Skills for Transformational School and District Leaders* (Solution Tree, 2019).

In their introduction, Muhammad and Cruz remind readers that "the most vital assets in an organization are the human resources." This book takes education leaders step by step through the process of gaining trust and support for their vision. Chapters cover the topics of gaining cognitive investment from staff, establishing trust with staff, building staff capacity, and getting the desired results from staff. Anthony Muhammad gave an interview about this book on Principal Center Radio that you can find on YouTube at https://www.youtube.com/watch?v=31gdgN9PX5I.

Edwin H. Moore, *School Public Relations for Student Success* (Corwin, 2009).

Local media provides a bridge to families and communities during a culture change at your school. Edwin H. Moore provides a step-by-step guide to delivering focused content to media that delivers the message you want to send. The book includes checklists, Q&A sessions with experienced education communicators, and ideas for public relations activities with employees, parents, students, and volunteers. One chapter focuses on public relations activities with diverse populations and another focuses on reaching out to senior community members.

Shelley Burgess and Beth Houf, *Lead Like a PIRATE: Make School Amazing for Your Staff and Students* (Dave Burgess Consulting, 2017).

Shelley Burgess and Beth Houf offer strategies for "dramatically transforming culture and building schools where students and staff run to get in, not out." PIRATE is their mnemonic for harness passion and encourage risk-taking, immerse yourself in the work that makes the biggest impact on learning, build rapport and relationships grounded in trust, analyze lessons and ask great questions to provide rich feedback that moves learning forward, transform school culture, and lead with enthusiasm. Part I describes the PIRATE model, Part II provides strategies for building leadership capacity at your school, Part III describes a coaching model that will help you offer and encourage feedback in an environment of trust, and Part IV offers tips and strategies for improving your leadership style.

3

What the Two Rules Teach Students

Learn to hear what a student cannot say.
—Whitney, a Fall Ridge student

In Chapter 2, I showed how the two rules are a promise to students: our school is a place where you will feel good and feel safe. In this chapter and Chapter 4, you will see me working with students to help them use the two rules to develop social and emotional skills. The issues that brought them to my office were not trivial. They were at the beginning of a journey of learning about issues people grapple with throughout their lives. Some were learning hard lessons about consent, some were learning about friendship, some were learning to control their tempers, some were learning how to handle losing face, some were learning how to be a trusted person.

A big strength of the two rules system is that each conversation is framed in a way that shows students how the rules benefit *them*. Instead of focusing on blame, condemnation, and punishment, my conversations with students facing problems showed them how their choices had the power to influence the outcomes they experienced. These conversations showed students how in each moment they had the power to make a choice that would help them or make life more difficult for them. Make no mistake; this is not a system about coddling students and excusing their behavior. I always held students to the highest standards of behavior and expected them to meet them. But when a student didn't or couldn't meet those standards, it was important for them to understand why and it was important for me to provide resources and support to help them get to the point where they could.

The two-rules conversations you see below show students in the process of acquiring cognitive and social skills they would need in adulthood. The earlier young people can acquire these skills, the better. And sadly, in our economically devastated community, many parents and caregivers had so many problems of their own that they weren't able to model these skills or teach them to the children they were responsible for. A two-rules framework that complements a disciplinary system creates an environment for learning life skills as well as academic skills.

Seeing Situations from Another Person's Perspective

Developing an open mind at a young age is a strength that will serve students well throughout their lives. Learning to appreciate the experiences of other people and give them opportunities to express themselves creates a richer context for all members of a community. Understanding the views of people who have viewpoints that differ from ours is a cornerstone of democracy. It is important for students to learn that when people can discuss their views openly, they can begin to agree on some things and disagree on others without fear or hostility.

Terra was an eighth-grade student who was struggling to understand how to navigate through her days and feelings. Her relationship with her mother had always been toxic. Terra had bonded with an older couple who were like grandparents to her. Both were retired educators who had known Terra's parents for years. Terra's mother and this couple had agreed informally that Terra would live with them because

Terra's relationship with her was so turbulent. The couple had become a source of stability and support for Terra.

I had been an administrator in Terra's elementary school, so by the time she got to the end of her eighth-grade year, she had been working with the two-rules system for four years. She had gained the skills she needed to process information and solve problems. But she had a lot to process—coping with raging hormones, figuring out who she was, processing the rift with her mother, and adjusting to a new living situation. Plus she was about to leave middle school and begin high school. That would put her in a pool of students she didn't know in a building that had a different culture and a different set of rules. It would also increase the pressure to start planning for her future.

So on the day her class went on a trip at the end of the year to celebrate their success, Terra had a lot going on. During the exuberance of the trip, Terra made some unwise choices. She approached other girls inappropriately and was placing maxi-pads on them. Her approaches were both verbal and physical. As soon as they got back, the lead teacher for her grade came to me and said, "You need to speak to Terra."

The couple Terra was living with had influential positions in the community. Staff at my school worried that the prominence of this couple in our city would make it difficult for me to deal with this tricky situation. But I was the same person with everyone I interacted with. I said the same things, followed the same actions, and asked the same questions whether I was with a custodian, superintendent, or the mayor. In addition, I had built relationships with Terra and all of her family. I knew that the issue would be resolved correctly regardless of who Terra's caregivers were.

After the class trip, the team leader for Terra's grade sent her to my office. When she arrived, I looked at her and she looked at me. When I began to speak, she stopped me.

"Mrs. Yoho, you do not need to say anything. I can talk about it. I was part of the problem today. The girls are right. I did all of the things they are saying and I know how they saw it. I should not have done those things and I know I should have asked the questions. I was not thinking about it. It was the end of the year and I had a lot inside me."

"Thank you, Terra. You write up your statement and I will get their statements so everyone will be clear about what happened. I know you are struggling with many things, but you know the expectations."

"I do."

Terra had allowed the exuberant feelings of being on a class trip to override the two-rules skills she had learned. However, she had built the skills she needed to apply the two rules to her situation. She had the tools to take responsibility for her actions and to understand the result of her actions. Terra had a consequence because in a heady environment, she forgot the crucial step of making sure of others' feelings. This all-important social skill is covered by the two rules: Will this make the other person feel good? Will it make them feel safe? Terra knew that if she had stopped to ask those questions, she would have behaved differently.

Becoming Aware of How to Be Safe

The two-rules philosophy does not replace the practices schools have about safety. Every school has policies and procedures for multiple situations, including storms, fires, riding the bus, and how students should act at school. The two rules help students understand the thought process that goes into these practices and the importance of always thinking about safety.

I wanted students to think about safety as a very personal topic that was about their own welfare instead of thinking about it as an annoying category in the student handbook. The young people in my school faced life-and-death issues that could rise up to confront them at any moment. More than once when I answered the phone, the person on the other end of the line told me about an accident that had taken the life of a student. One of our students was abducted and killed during my years as an educator. Many students lived in homes where violence could erupt in an instant.

I couldn't control the issues they faced outside the walls of my school, but I could show students what safety looked like while they were inside them. I could show them how unthinking, reactive actions could quickly escalate to violence and how they could learn to interrupt that cycle.

Running and pushing in the hallways may seem innocent, but if someone is having a bad day, a situation can escalate very quickly. Some of the hallways in our building were not wide enough for multiple classes to pass and if someone was shoved and they fell hard into the lockers, they could be injured. Another space where safety was key was the gym. Dodgeball was my pet peeve. I didn't like it; I thought it encouraged bullying. When we had dodgeball on Fridays, we always had aggressive behaviors over these games.

While Cody was walking down the hallway, Ethan pushed him down. When Cody was pushed, he fell into a third boy, Jared, who did not see Ethan push him. Jared pulled Cody up and punched him. Now we had three people involved in an unsafe situation. We were able to get the three boys into the conference room to discuss what had happened and gather information from those who had witnessed the incident.

In a meeting with more than one student, it is critical to begin by reminding everyone about how important it is for every person to feel good and feel safe. In this case, I began by reviewing the safety protocols for our school. I then asked each boy what he had seen and how he understood the situation. I reminded them that each person would have a chance to speak and be heard.

It is important to go back to the beginning of a situation. In this case, what happened in the hallway didn't begin in the hallway. It began in the gym. When emotions rise in the discussion—and they will—stop and ask which emotion is speaking right now. This helps students identify their feelings. Recognizing emotions is the first step in learning how to control them, to avoid being reactive.

I always established the guidelines for talking in this group setting:

1. One person will talk at a time.

2. Listen to what is being said.

3. If you do not agree, you can state why when it is your turn to talk.

Here is the conversation I had with the three boys.

    Me: Ethan, what happened?

Ethan: In dodgeball, he threw the ball at me on purpose to get me out first. He hit me hard in the back of the head and you are not supposed to hit in the head.

    Me: Cody, did you hit Ethan?

  Cody: I hit him, but I did not hit him on purpose in the head. It is dodgeball, and you are supposed to get your opponents out.

Ethan: I know everyone knows dodgeball is not my favorite game. You are supposed to get people out by hitting them.

    Me: Do you really think Cody did it on purpose?

Ethan: I don't know.

    Me: Do you think your actions in the hallway were safe?

Ethan: No.

    Me: Why?

Ethan: Well, I pushed Cody and he fell into Jared. Cody could have hit his head on the lockers, and Jared could have been hurt too. It made Jared mad.

    Me: Jared, what happened?

Jared: Cody pushed into me, and it made me mad. I don't like people to touch me.

    Me: Do you think it was on purpose?

Jared: Not now.

    Me: Do you think what you did was safe for everyone?

Jared: Well, I guess not.

    Me: What was not safe?

Jared: Well, I should have stopped to ask questions in my mind first. I should have seen if he was okay. Then I could have found out what happened. I just reacted by being mad.

Me: Okay, so do we all see, hear, and understand about the safety issues here? Do we see how we can make better choices? Dodgeball is a game played for fun. If you have a question, ask to talk about it. If you are not able to talk about it in gym, ask your next classroom teacher if you can speak to someone in the office about it. Safety in the hallways is important because we are in close proximity to each other. Having safe hands and feet and quiet voices helps us transition safely to the next area when we are by other classrooms. We want everyone to feel safe and be safe and especially we want ourselves to also have those same things. When we are not safe, we choose to be part of the problem and we want to be part of the solution. Keeping ourselves physically safe is not the only way to be safe, so help out by also feeling safe by the words we use, how we include everyone, and the way we treat others.

I often used the story of six blind men and the elephant to help students understand that in each situation, other people will see it from a different perspective than their own. In the story, six blind men encounter an elephant. Because it is so large, each man can touch only a part of it. As a result, each person identifies it as something different from what the others perceive. They begin arguing because each one believes that they are right. If they could have pooled their knowledge, they might have been able to perceive the whole animal together.

In such meetings, I would remind students of the importance of gathering information before responding to a situation. Doing that task provides space for emotions to cool down and logic and curiosity to come to the forefront. I would tell students that when we don't stop to ask important questions, we miss out because we don't see the entire picture. When we understand a situation from the perspective of other people, we are ready to make good choices. This is the framework I used in the meeting with Ethan, Cody, and Jared. During our conversation, each boy began to look at what happened from the perspective of the other boys. They realized that if they had taken a moment to gather information, they could have avoided a conflict that escalated.

Learning to Ask Two-Rules Questions When Faced with a Problem

Sometimes students' solutions to their problems led them into the legal system. I always worked intensively with those students. I wanted them to see that they had the power to make different choices, to find different solutions to their problems. I wanted them to understand that although their first attempt to address an issue had failed, they could try again and do better. The two rules gave students opportunities to talk through their experiences and develop reliable mental habits that would lead to good solutions to the problems they would face during their life's journey.

Deandra was a seventh grader. We were about forty days into the school year. We had worked on safety for the first thirty days of school and we were just beginning to talk about feeling good. What does feeling good mean? In our high-poverty school, feeling good meant having something clean to wear. For middle school girls, especially girls of color living in poverty, changing clothes in a locker room is a big deal. When you look at the situation with what you believe is no other choice, you make a poor one. That is what happened with Deandra. She wanted to feel good, so she stole a package of underwear. She was caught and the store owner called the police. When the police asked her who she wanted them to call, she gave them my name.

I had a good relationship with our police department and they were aware of what I was doing at Fall Ridge with the two rules. When they called me, they asked me how I thought they should proceed. I said they should take her home and let her keep the underwear. I would pay the merchant and talk with Deandra about a way she could pay me back. We agreed that she would make a court appearance. I worked closely with the state attorney's office and officials in the court system to advocate for Deandra and to reach a solution with the court that would not harm her future.

The outcome of her court appearance was that she was referred to Peer Court, a nonprofit that does interventions when a juvenile commits a low-level crime. A judge refers the young person to Peer Court as an alternative to creating a criminal record. The court is run by students from around the district who serve as lawyers and jury members who decide what the consequences for the crime will be. The consequences often include community service and/or an apology letter to parents or other people the young person has harmed.

The day after I spoke with the police, Deandra returned to school and my secretary asked her to come see me. This is the conversation I had with Deandra.

> **Me:** Deandra, why did you steal the underwear?
>
> **Deandra:** I did not have any clean underwear and I needed clean ones.
>
> **Me:** Did you ask yourself questions about how you could get clean ones?
>
> **Deandra:** Well, we do not have a washer or dryer. I would have to go to laundromat and it costs money. So does the soap.
>
> **Me:** What other ideas did you have?
>
> **Deandra:** I only thought I did not have money to wash clothes or buy new ones. So I thought I just would take them.
>
> **Me:** Did you ask yourself if that would make you feel good?
>
> **Deandra:** I thought at least I would have clean underwear.
>
> **Me:** Did you think what would happen when they needed to be washed?
>
> **Deandra:** I did not think about that.
>
> **Me:** Did you think about if it was safe to steal?
>
> **Deandra:** No.

Me: What do you think now?

Deandra: I think asking more questions and talking with someone else like an adult would be better before you do something. It did not solve my problem; I just have another one.

Me: Yes, you know the social worker or any of us can help you with figuring out how to handle getting clean clothes. We even have a washer and dryer here at the school. I am sure we can figure out how to problem-solve this issue with you. I think you will be able to help teach the kids at Peer Court how to ask questions to problem-solve. How do you feel?

Deandra: I know I can help them. I like the questions and finding solutions.

At Peer Court, Deandra took full responsibility for her action and told the students who were serving that day about the questioning process of the two-rules framework. She pointed out that if she had stopped to ask the two questions—Will this make me feel good? Will it make me feel safe?—she would have realized that her problem had other solutions and that she needed the help of a trusted adult to help her find a better one than stealing. She used her time at Peer Court to tell students from other schools how the two rules worked at our school. Her peers sentenced her to community service and she was able to avoid a juvenile criminal record. She never had another incident that got her into trouble with the law.

This event illustrates a number of ways the principal of a two-rules school can support students. I knew that Deandra had acted out of need and a sense of panic about not having clean clothes. As was the case with many of her classmates, poverty had put her in a position where she was trying to cope with adult concerns without the resources or guidance to do it successfully. Because of my good relationships with the police and with court officials, I was able to negotiate a consequence for her based on compassion and trust in my judgment. Instead of taking the first step on the school-to-prison pipeline, Deandra had an empowering experience that enabled her to demonstrate to her peers that she felt remorse and that she had a mental framework in place—the two rules—that would prevent her from reoffending. At Peer Court, she told students from around the district how the two rules operated at Fall Ridge and how they had changed her school to a place she wanted to be.

Learning to Be Responsive Instead of Reactive

This is the issue we worked on the most with students. Acquiring this skill takes daily work and years to master. Even adults have difficulty implementing this practice sometimes. However, once a person has formed the habit of asking questions before they respond and taking the time to cool down, they will have better results in any situation. One of the first steps in this process is learning what buttons we have and working to master the habit of taking a breath when people push those buttons. This is not easy for young people to do, and they require many reminders and lots of support as they learn. In the example below, Sean was a talker who liked to be seen and heard when he was in the classroom. One day his low impulse control disrupted his class and landed him in my office. The first task was to learn what had happened from Sean's perspective. Then I could use questions to help him consider the perspective of the other people in his classroom.

Me:	Sean, what happened?
Sean:	Mr. Martin sent me to your office because he is mad at me.
Me:	Why do you think he is mad at you?
Sean:	Because he got all red in the face and raised his voice at me. He told me to get out and to come see you.
Me:	Why did he want you to leave the classroom?
Sean:	I'm not sure. I guess because I kept sayin' stuff.
Me:	What would saying stuff mean?

Sean: Well, he was telling us a story about baseball. He started talking about Cardinals and Cubs. I like the Cubs. I told him that when he was telling the story. Then Caleb said he liked the Cardinals. I started to argue with Caleb and then other people said stuff. Mr. Martin finally got us to all settle down. Then, in the story he had the colors of the uniforms wrong. The Cubs were wearing red and they don't wear red. I tried to tell him that and others agreed with me. People started talking about how the Cardinals wear red. Then Mr. Martin told me to get out and come see you.

Me: Well, if we think about the two rules, how would we apply them in this situation. Mr. Martin sent you out of the classroom to come see me. Was it because he didn't feel safe or because he thought others didn't feel safe?

Sean: No. I can say that right away. I didn't do anything to make anyone not feel safe.

Me: Well, is it because Mr. Martin didn't feel good or others didn't feel good?

Sean: I'm not sure about that one. I was interrupting a lot and people were joining in with me, so this meant we weren't getting to our lesson. I guess Mr. Martin wasn't feeling very good. His face was very red.

Me: Okay, maybe we're on to something. Do you like it when someone is interrupting you?

Sean: No. It's hard to get your thoughts out there if you are always interrupted. Maybe this is the reason I am here.

Me: I see. Now that you have told me the story, can you see and hear Mr. Martin's point of view?

Sean: I don't know.

Me: He was telling all of you a story, right?

Sean: Yeah.

Me: Did he say it was based on a true story?

Sean: No.

Me: You just heard Cubs and Cardinals so you connected it to the real teams you know.

Sean: Yes.

Me: I think that is great! I like how you were able to connect with the story to something you know. Do you think it helped to interrupt the story to share at that time?

Sean: Well, it just came to my mind and I was excited about the story. I wanted everyone to know I liked the Cubs.

Me: I am so glad you were excited about the story, but do you think interrupting the story was the best time or waiting until the story was over to share all of your thoughts would be better?

Sean: I guess I should have waited, because now I missed out on the story. When I said something, everyone else did too!

Me: Yes, then everyone was talking about stuff and the story was not being heard. Not being able to read the story—I am guessing that frustrated Mr. Martin. I believe that is why you are here with me.

Sean: Now that I am thinking about it, I get mad when I am not able to talk when I want to talk.

Me: We all have little buttons that make us angry like being interrupted, which makes us react to situations. Do you think you were respectful or pushing a button by interrupting?

Sean: I was not respectful and probably pushing a button, because I did it again.

Me: You've done a great job of thinking through this issue. I am sure we can work it out so you can hear the story and then you can do the assignment Mr. Martin gave the class about the story. But what do you think your next step could be with Mr. Martin?

Sean: I can apologize to Mr. Martin for being part of the problem today. I can tell him how I can improve and we can talk through it.

The focus of this conversation was helping Sean identify what happened and how he was feeling in the moment when Mr. Martin sent him to my office. That helped him identify how his behavior was affecting his teacher and the other students in his class. He walked out of my office with an understanding that not being able to talk whenever he wanted to made him angry. This was perhaps the first time he had verbalized that connection. That was something he came to understand on his own as we talked. I didn't tell him that. He figured it out for himself, so he saw making a plan for finding different ways of behaving as his project rather than something that I or Mr. Martin imposed on him. He was ready to take responsibility for his actions and work with his teacher on strategies for learning how to control his impulse to speak when it wasn't his turn.

As I talked with him, I verbalized the cognitive skill he was using—connecting what he was learning with what he already knew. I wanted him to hear that I saw that he was doing a good job of developing a key skill he needed for learning. Now he needed to take his development one step further by learning how to wait for his turn to speak in a classroom situation. This was a framework I used every day with Fall Ridge students: "Look at the skills you're using! You're doing great! Now let's think about how you can move ahead to the next step."

After my conversation with Sean, I spoke with Mr. Martin about identifying his personal triggers and about having strategies in place for maintaining an even demeanor when a student acted in a way that activated them. Every teacher and every administrator has triggers. All of us are carrying baggage from our past. The important thing is to identify our triggers and learn to respond in different ways so we can maintain a stable, predictable environment when we're interacting with students.

Soon after this event, Mr. Martin ate lunch with Sean so Sean could hear the full story he told the class. He talked with him about the fact that when we hear a story, we may hear common names that we associate with real things. As I had, he complimented Sean on using that skill of association. But he helped him take that skill to the next level by distinguishing between what he knew to be true in real life and a narrative that he heard in a story. Instead of focusing on punishment, both Mr. Martin and I used this incident to help Sean become familiar with a new critical thinking skill.

Developing Compassion for Others

When the culture of the school is focused on the core foundation of support for others, compassion is an element that appears very quickly. Children who are experiencing hardships and struggles quickly learn to identify with the needs of others. They understand the desire for compassion.

Sammy was a special needs student with a very low IQ who desperately wanted to be part of the group. He had great difficulty controlling his emotions and was given to angry outbursts. He was not in regular classrooms, but he was able to attend P.E. and other elective classes with the support of paraprofessionals. He had the biggest smile most of the time, but he could flip very quickly to anger. He desperately wanted to participate in activities that other sixth grade boys did, but he didn't have the social skills to do well in groups.

One of the things he loved to do was play basketball. He could not be part of the regular team because he did not have the social skills everyone else had and his behaviors did not guarantee that he could be part of such a large group setting for extended times. However, when our intervention team decided we would use basketball as part of his goals, everyone was all in.[1] Sammy worked hard with me and with the school social worker on specific behaviors and made some gains in terms of interacting with other students. However, he needed a structured situation in order to function well.

I asked the basketball coach to talk with the team about Sammy and his great desire to play with them. He told them that Sammy was working very hard on earning enough points on his behavior development chart to enable him to come to a practice. He explained that Sammy was working especially hard on learning to ask the two questions—Will this make me/others feel good? Will this make me/others feel safe?—before he responded to a situation. This reminded the team that they were all working on acquiring the same skills. Everyone was at their own level in their quest to master this skill.

One great day Sammy had finally earned enough points and he was able to go to a basketball practice. The boys welcomed and encouraged him as Sammy played on a team for the first time. They said things like, "Great pass, Sammy." and "Good shot!" When he had earned the right to attend a game, I saw the boys ask their coach to put Sammy in. They cheered for him when he got the ball. He even made a basket. These were my sixth graders showing me they were coming to understand what it meant to be compassionate for others and what it meant to work together as a team.

Learning How to Solve Problems

As educators, you will find many opportunities to reinforce a solution-seeking mindset in your interactions with students. I loved teaching teens and preteens to change how they viewed problems. My mantra of "Do you want to be part of the problem or do you want to be part of the solution?" reminded students that solutions were there for them to find. Looking at a situation through the lens of possible solutions helped them think about the choices they had. I firmly believe that when people choose to look for solutions instead of seeing only problems, the choices they make will contribute to feeling good and feeling safe. Students who see this approach in action in their school and who have opportunities to see themselves as leaders who solve problems will become adults who contribute to greater cooperation at work, in their communities, and in the broader world. Developing the daily practices that lead to a solution-focused mindset at an early age will help them cope with current and future challenges.

As I worked with students who were struggling with problems, I helped them take the first step: identifying their problem. I showed them that asking questions and talking about the problem often brings out details that lead to new perspectives and possibilities. Several books that present ways to approach problems have been published for young people since my years as a school principal. One is *What Do You Do With a Problem?* by Kobi Yamada, which is written for young children. Another is *Pink Bat: Turning Problems into Solutions* by Michael McMillan.[2]

Brittany was a sixth grader who I had known for a few years because I had been an administrator in her elementary school. She was familiar with the two rules. Every morning during announcements, Brittany heard the mantra question of the school: "Do you want to be part of the problem or do you want to be part of the solution?" She knew that she had a problem that she didn't know how to solve. Because she trusted me, she made an appointment to see me in my office.

We had worked with students in her elementary school on friendship skills, and Brittany had a core group of close friends who had come to Fall Ridge with her. When she got to middle school, she encountered students she didn't know who had come to Fall Ridge from other elementary schools. She soon found herself in a social situation she wasn't comfortable with. It was something that happened every day and she didn't know what to do about it. Every day when she was at her locker, a girl she didn't know made a point of also going to her locker, which was next to Brittany's. While Brittany was talking with her friends, this girl would stand nearby and watch Brittany. This was annoying Brittany and making her angry.

My office had a table where I could sit with students as I talked with them. This was important for making students more comfortable. I wasn't an authority figure sitting behind a desk. I didn't even sit across the table from them. Instead, I sat beside them, showing them with my body positioning that we were working together to understand a situation. Brittany sat down and I pulled up a chair next to her.

I asked her to define her problem. She responded, "Julie is bugging me every day!"

In this situation, I wanted to model for her how asking the two-rules questions would lead to more and more questions that would help her understand her feelings more clearly and, equally important, lead her to see the situation from Julie's perspective.

> **Me:** You have identified the problem, but clarify "bugging" so you can solve the core problem. What does it mean to you to be bugged every day? Once you clarify the meaning, then you can begin to ask questions to yourself and also think about the other person. So tell me more about how Julie is bugging you. When does this happen?
>
> **Brittany:** It happens every morning! I am at my locker getting stuff out for the day and I am talking with my friends. And as soon as she sees me at my locker she comes over and stands in front of her locker too. She isn't even getting stuff out; she's just pretending. And she stands there and watches us while I am talking to my friends.
>
> **Me:** Oh. So who are your friends that you're talking to?
>
> **Brittany:** You know, my friends from last year. Max and Tamara and Terry. We always have a lot to talk about.
>
> **Me:** Okay. So does Julie bug you at other times of the day?
>
> **Brittany:** Yes! It seems like every time I turn around, she is there watching me. I don't like it.

At this point, the situation was clear to me. Both Brittany and Julie were grappling with friendship issues. Brittany thought that her network of close friends was set and that her friendship skills were fine. She didn't realize that there are different levels of friendship and that it's okay to have friends who aren't in an intimate circle of close friends. Julie lacked the skills to initiate conversations that might lead to friendship and was struggling to make friends in a new environment in which some friendship networks were already established. I began modeling questions for Brittany that would help her work through this situation.

> **Me:** So let's start with the two questions. Do you feel good when you and Julie are at your lockers?
>
> **Brittany:** No. I don't like it.
>
> **Me:** "Okay, so you don't feel good. Is there anything you could do to change that so you would feel good and Julie would also feel good? For example, do you ever say anything to Julie?
>
> **Brittany:** No.
>
> **Me:** Hm. And does Julie ever say anything to you?
>
> **Brittany:** No! That's the problem! She just stares at me and never says anything!
>
> **Me:** Okay, let's move to the second question. Do you feel safe when you and Julie are at your lockers?
>
> **Brittany:** Well, yes, I guess so. All of my friends are nearby and I want to talk to them.
>
> **Me:** So let's look at the second part of the feeling safe question. Do you think Julie feels safe when you are talking with your friends and nobody is talking to her?

Brittany paused for a moment, then shrugged. "I don't know! How am I supposed to know if she feels safe?"

Despite her defensive answer, I could see that she was starting to think about her problem in a different way.

I had a big whiteboard in my office. I liked to use it to help visualize what students and I talked about. I asked Brittany to go to the whiteboard so she could draw a diagram of her problem. This was an important step in many of my two-rules conversations with students. When they diagrammed their problem, they were thinking and talking and doing at the same time. Those three activities engaged different parts of their brain as they worked through an issue.

I said, "I like to use the whiteboard because it will help you see what this problem looks like. We need to start looking at how this affects you, how it affects her, how it affects everyone. So draw a circle in the middle of the whiteboard and write inside it what your understanding of the problem is now that we've been talking about it a bit."

Brittany drew a circle and wrote, "She is following me everywhere."

"Good," I said. "Now let's get more specific. Where is she following you? Draw smaller circles to the right of the big one and label the places, then draw arrows from the big circle to the little circles."

Brittany drew three circles and wrote "Locker," "Bathroom," and "Lunchroom."

I looked at the diagram (see Figure 3.1) and said, "Hmm. I notice that these are all locations inside the school. I see that you didn't say that she follows you to the bus. Is that because she rides a different bus?"

Brittany: Yes, she lives on the other side of town. I ride home with some of my other friends on the bus and we usually walk the rest of the way home together.

Me: I see. Have you talked to her about riding on the bus and what she does on the way home? Does she have brothers and sisters?

Brittany: I don't know.

Me: Oh. So you don't know if she talks to anyone when she is riding the bus. Have you noticed if she talks to anyone at school? Do you see her talking to anyone in the lunchroom or in the hallways or in the bathroom?

There was a pause in our conversation while Brittany thought about this. I waited for her to speak. I could see that she was mentally going through the times when she saw Julie and processing my question.

After a fairly long pause, Brittany slowly said, "No, I don't think so."

I said, "Okay. What about in classrooms? Do you see her talking to other kids or to a teacher?"

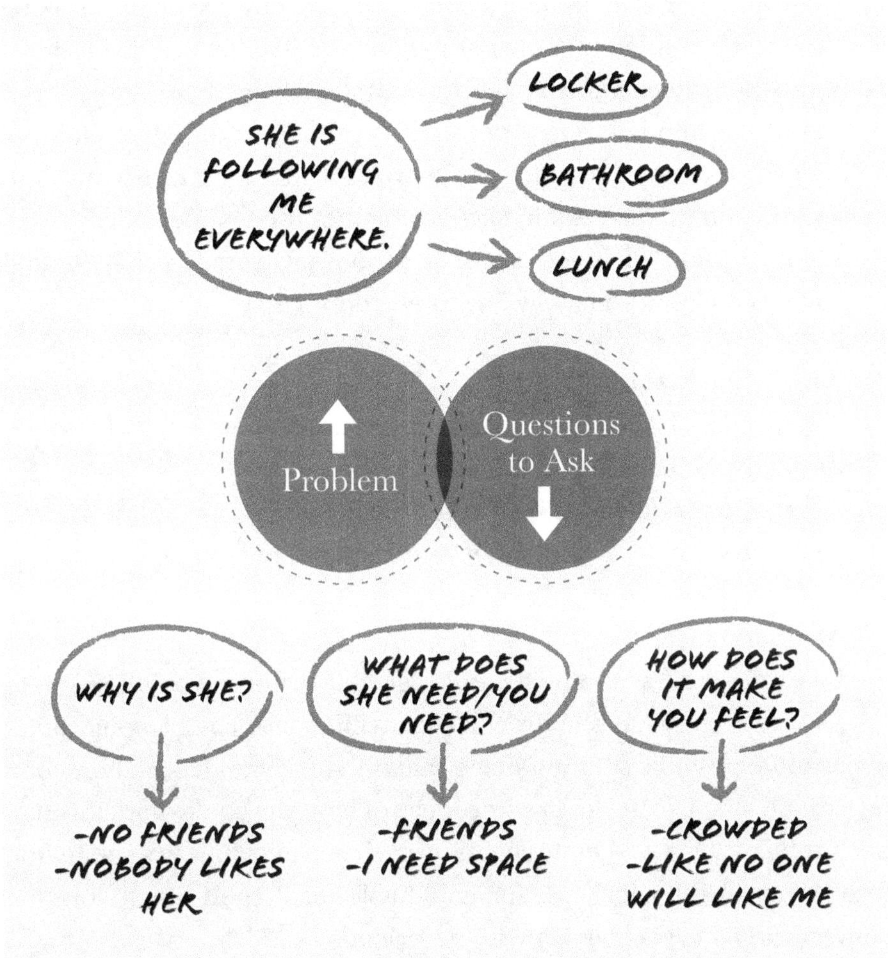

Figure 3.1. *Brittany's whiteboard*

Brittany responded, "No, I guess I don't."

I asked, "Brittany, how do you feel when you are talking to your friends?"

Brittany said, "I feel great! I love talking to my friends. It makes me feel really good."

I answered, "You are telling me that you have never seen Julie talking to a friend. Let's think about what it would be like for you if you didn't talk to anybody during the day."

There was another long pause. Brittany finally said, "I guess it probably doesn't feel very good for her." There was another pause while Brittany processed this. We sat in silence together for a while.

Finally I said, "Okay, let's get back to your problem. You have stated that Julie is bugging you. Now how is she doing that?"

Brittany: She is staring at me.

Me: Okay, but you've never said anything to her.

Brittany: No, I haven't.

Me: So how can she know that she is bugging you? How are you solving your problem if you're not talking to her?"

Another pause.

I waited for a few moments, then asked if Brittany would like me to take a picture of what she drew on the whiteboard so she could think about some possible solutions. She said no, she wanted to sit there for a few minutes and write down some ideas of how she could work through her problem. One of her thoughts was that when Julie was standing next to her at their lockers, she could ask her if she'd like to join the conversation she was having with her friends.

The interactions between them began slowly. They began exchanging a few words in the morning and the situation became less awkward for both of them. Brittany eventually told Julie that she had been uncomfortable when Julie stood there without participating in the conversations she was having with her friends. She told Julie that she felt that it was her fault because she should have been asking her if she needed anything instead of assuming that Julie was being intentionally rude. Julie responded that she was partly to blame, but she had been afraid to say anything because she didn't know anybody and didn't have a lot of friends.

Brittany and Julie never became close friends, but they worked together to create a friendly environment that felt more comfortable to them. They both began to learn the skill of initiating a conversation with someone they didn't know. And Brittany learned not to assume bad intentions without talking with someone to learn where they were coming from. Brittany's problem turned into a good experience in which both she and Julie learned social and emotional skills.

Meanwhile, I spoke with Julie's team about her situation and the team began making sure that Julie was paired with students she could talk with in classroom situations. They also incorporated friendship skills in the curriculum in subtle ways.

Supporting Brittany as she broke her problem into smaller components helped her learn how to ask more and more questions until she could see her problem in a new way. When I asked her if she had ever seen Julie talking with someone in all of the places where Brittany felt Julie was bugging her, something shifted in Brittany's thinking. She moved from looking at her problem only from her perspective to begin thinking about the situation from Julie's perspective. She realized that Julie probably wasn't feeling good and might not even be feeling safe. The two rules were gateway ideas that helped her go deeper until she could see how she could handle the situation differently.

Taking Responsibility for Actions

It is difficult for many people to admit when they are wrong. Children know that when they do so, they may miss out on something or pay some other consequence. Developing teenagers are trying to figure out many things. Their bodies are changing and hormones are affecting everything they think and do. Many times, we educators will encounter raw situations where an unthinking young person does something that plunges them into the legal system in a way that could haunt them for the rest of their lives.

These are situations where strong relationships with families will help all the people involved. Strong relationships and bonds of trust—a belief on the part of the student and their parents or caregivers that you are there to help—will help you during difficult conversations. Even though my school had over 600 students, I made it a priority to get to know each student. I worked to get to know their parents. I made home visits. I welcomed parents into the school. I established good working relations *before* a crisis occurred. So whenever my secretary told me that the parent of a student urgently needed to talk to me, I welcomed the parent gladly. Both the parent and I knew that we were on the same side—the side of the student. We did not have to wade through an adversarial relationship to get to the point where we could work together to help a young person we both cared about.

One day the mother of an outstanding student came to see me. Cameron was always helping, doing many positive things around the school. Everyone trusted him to do important jobs. The staff and I knew that Cameron's parents had gone through a divorce and that he had struggled with this, but we had not seen any changes in his behavior at school.

His mother came into my office, shut the door, and began to cry. I was not expecting that at all and was not sure what was happening. "Mrs. Yoho, the worst thing has happened to my son," she said. "His father reported him to the Department of Children and Family Services for child endangerment for touching his stepsister."

I said, "I am listening to you. Where is he now?"

"He is in the car," she replied. "I wanted to come in first to talk to you. We have to go to the DCFS office at 10 o'clock. They are going to take his statement and then they are going to do an investigation. I am not sure about any of this stuff. He is a good boy. I do not know what is going to happen to him."

"Okay," I said. "Let's get settled down first because being upset will not help him. So how about if you bring him in so I can speak with him and then you can go to the meeting at DCFS. I know this is upsetting to you, but if we can hold our emotions together in front of him it will work out better for everyone involved." Here is the conversation Cameron and I had.

Me:	Your mom told me a little bit about your situation, but I would like you to tell me about it.
Cameron:	Well, I was asked to babysit for my stepsister so my dad and stepmother could go out. I did not mean for anything to happen. I was playing with her and tickling her.
Me:	Can I ask you if you can reflect back on your story and use our two-rules questions? Think back over your situation before you go to your meeting and use the two-rules steps to help you with telling your story.
Cameron:	Okay.
Me:	I will give you time. Cameron, I know what kind of student and person you are. We all have worked on many things here at school to address many issues that will come up in our lives. These steps and questions we work on help us in our daily lives too.
Cameron:	Mrs. Yoho, I was part of the problem.
Me:	How were you part of the problem and why are you saying that now?
Cameron:	My dad and stepmother trusted me to take care of my little sister and I did not make her feel safe or good.
Me:	What do you mean?

Cameron:	She told me to stop tickling her and I didn't. I kept tickling her and I touched her in places I know I should not be touching.
Me:	Have you done that before?
Cameron:	No, I was not thinking. I was just playing around. But if I think about it now, I know I was wrong.
Me:	Do you think you would do that again?
Cameron:	Never, not to anyone. I know I have to accept the consequences of what I did.
Me:	You will, and I will speak on your behalf. I do want you to go through the steps of what you did. You have said that you didn't make your stepsister feel good or safe. Now you have to talk with people at the Department of Children and Family Services about what happened. It is their job to make sure that all children feel good and feel safe in their homes. We don't know yet what the consequences will be for your actions. However, I do know that telling the truth and the entire truth is what is always needed in everything we say and do.

I questioned myself intensely about this situation. I had never gone to DCFS to support a student who had been accused of inappropriate touching before. I had always gone to support the victims. Was I making the right decision? Was I seeing things correctly? Was this incident the tip of an iceberg? Was Cameron more troubled by all of the family upheaval he was undergoing than anyone realized? It was so important to make sure that any action I took was for the benefit of children and young people.

In this case, I knew Cameron well and I knew his family. Cameron had been my student in elementary school, so by the time he got to middle school, he had been using the two-rules process for several years. With repetition, he had learned how to use it to analyze his behavior and he was taking responsibility for his actions. DCFS decided that Cameron's visits with his stepsister would be monitored for a year, which was the right move. Nothing like this ever happened again.

Learning to Be Proactive When Facing a Problem

An important skill I worked to help students develop was knowing when it is time to ask for help. So many students in our building were dealing with problems that were overwhelming, problems they couldn't cope with on their own. And then there were times when a peaceful relationship would suddenly become volatile. Those were times when students definitely needed help, and I frequently reminded them that my door was always open to them.

I was usually in my office at least an hour before students arrived. One morning, Lucia and her parents arrived at my office to speak to me shortly after I got there. I heard the doorbell for the front door to the school ring because it sounded throughout the school; the janitorial staff had not turned it off yet.

I got up to push the camera button to see who it was. When I recognized them, I told them to come in and met them at the door. I invited them to come to my office as I saw the janitor coming around the corner. I waved at him to indicate it was okay.

Dad began to speak first. "Lucia told us last night that she had received a message from another girl that there would be a fight with her today. We are here with her early because she said she needed to talk with you before the day began."

"I appreciate you both taking time to bring her in this morning to speak to me," I replied. I turned to Lucia and this is the conversation that followed.

Me: Thank you, Lucia, for being proactive in working on a solution to this issue. You have identified the problem for me. A fight is something that could happen today. Please help me with the questions we ask when we identify a problem. Who does it involve?

Lucia: Who is me and Camila.

Me: The next question is what happened?

Lucia: We was on the bus going home. We got off the bus and when we were walking she tripped and fell. Everyone laughed, not just me. But she sent me a message last night that said we were going to fight today 'cause I was making fun of her.

Me: Did you reply back?

Lucia: Nope, I went and told my dad that I needed to go to the school early to talk to Mrs. Yoho.

Me: Okay, I need to also ask you if you sent messages to anyone else about this incident?

Lucia: Well, I did talk to her sister Daniela and the others who was with us walking. To find out why they were not getting messages from her.

Me: Now I want you to go back and think about walking home, but you are Camila. You trip and fall. What are you feeling, thinking, and needing?

Lucia: If I fell down, I know it would hurt. I would be mad if everyone was looking at me and laughing.

Me: Can you remember if your eyes met Camila's eyes while you were laughing?

Lucia: I don't know. Maybe.

Me: In the moment Camila fell down, did she feel good?

Lucia: No.

Me: Did Camila feel safe?

Lucia: No.

Me: Fighting is not the answer to solve the problem, but what could be?

Lucia: I know what we need to do. We need to all get together and tell her we are sorry. We should not have done that to her. We need to give her a hug.

Me: I think I can arrange for all of you to meet together, but remember that not everyone is willing to hear an apology or accept it. Sometimes it takes time. However, I will make sure there will not be any fighting today at school or on the bus and that you will get home safely today.

During the meeting we had, these girls worked out their problem. They were actually good friends and Lucia had been surprised at the rapid turn of events. In our meeting, with gentle prompting, Lucia was able to see the situation from Camila's point of view. Camila had lost face when she fell down and then it was made worse when her friends laughed at her. She believed that fighting Lucia was a quick way to get her image as a tough girl back in place. In the meeting, we explored other parts of Camila's identity, other things she was good at besides being tough. We made a list of things Camila was good at. The girls all contributed to the list: She is good at softball; she is great at math; in art she makes the best paintings; in P.E. she runs faster than most of the boys; she is the best sister; she is a great friend. The outcome of the meeting was that Lucia took responsibility for her action of participating in laughter and she gained a better understanding of what made her friend tick. And Camila gained a better understanding of herself. The two girls left the meeting arm-in-arm with a deeper sense of their friendship.

Developing a Sense of Self-Efficacy

Self-efficacy, a belief in oneself and what one can do, will build as students continue to acquire the skills that follow from using the two rules every day. When you have students over a period of time and can follow their accomplishments into adulthood, it is gratifying to see them grow.

Whitney was being raised by a single mother who had mental health issues. She took both Whitney and her younger brother to doctors frequently with false reports about their health. As a result, both children were taking medications they didn't need. The situation bordered on medical abuse, but there wasn't enough evidence to get DCFS involved. The mother would deny any report we passed along. By the second week of school, I had noticed Whitney. She was a girl with big eyes with a story she did not want anyone to know. If you made eye contact with her, she would look down. It was easy to tell that she was not feeling good or safe about anything.

She had put up a wall that was hard to tear down. Her mother had betrayed her trust so many times that it was almost impossible for her to trust any adult. She had missed many days of school and she was deeply depressed. We began our relationship with a few exchanges in the hallway. Then Whitney came to my office to talk several times. She didn't like one of the medications she was on and she didn't like the doctor she was seeing. I presented this information to Whitney's mother and gave her names of other doctors who would be happy to see Whitney. The mother rejected this information and refused to listen to what I had to say. She was opposed to any kind of intervention. That was all we could do as a school. The situation was frustrating for me and very difficult for Whitney.

During one of Whitney's visits to my office, I suggested that we begin a journal exchange. Whitney would write in her journal after school, then leave it on my desk in the morning when she arrived. I would read what she wrote, then respond with encouraging messages. Whitney would pick up the journal at the end of the school day from my secretary. In our exchanges, I focused on being a trusted adult who believed in her and was there to support her in a difficult situation.

I often wrote about the tools of two rules and reinforced the core principle of choices we make as a positive way to continue to move forward. I told her she was building on the two rules to become the person I knew she could be. Every day I reminded her that no one can take choices away from you and no one can stop you from believing in you. Every day I said to her, "I believe in you."

Helping students recognize the power they have is a big step. Kids involved in traumatic events, dysfunctional families, or abusive relationships sometimes will feel powerless. We worked with the truancy officer to build up support for Whitney coming to school. Whitney and I talked a lot about things she could control, since so much at home was out of her control. I reminded her that when someone said something that hurt her feelings, she could control how she responded. She could refuse to believe what that person said. She could write down their words, then crumple up the paper or rip it up and throw it away. She could try the strategy of saying "You are right" and seeing how the hurtful person responded to such a surprising response. I pointed out that every day she made the decision to get out of bed and every day she could build on that by making one more decision about something she could control. She could control how she listened in class and she could control her learning. I encouraged her to make a list of things she could control.

Whitney learned to problem-solve by using the two rules to handle the things she could control and to focus on the choices she could make. I made sure that I didn't miss a day of writing to her in that journal. Over the holiday break, I sent her a Christmas card to make sure she knew that our connection wasn't broken even though we weren't writing to each other. We wrote to each other every school day for a year. Then Whitney's family moved and I moved to a different position. Years later, she reached out to me to tell me she used those journals every day of her life to work through her issues. She kept them and still has them. The process helped her to continue to grow and develop. Whitney survived her traumatic childhood and went to nursing school. Today she is a nurse who is doing good work to heal from her childhood trauma. When she was a young teenager, she didn't have the words to say what her trauma was. But she did have the words to keep a line of communication open with a trusted adult and begin building problem-solving skills that would serve her well.

Conclusion

Most of the students in the examples I gave in this chapter had been students in elementary schools where I was an administrator, so they had been learning how to use the two rules for several years by the time they entered Fall Ridge. They had gone through the process of internalizing the two rules and were able to use them to understand their situations and their feelings better.

The length of time they had been working with the two rules is an important point. It takes at least one year of daily reminders for a middle school student to incorporate the two rules into the way they see the world. They will need to hear the framing question—Do you want to be part of the problem or do you want to be part of the solution?—every single day. They will need to be reminded to ask the two questions—Will this make me/them feel good? Will this make me/them feel safe?—even more frequently, especially when they act in ways that break one of these rules. It will take them most of a year to fully internalize these questions and use them to stop and think before they act.

Another point to note is that even students who have internalized the two rules will need support and modeling from a trusted adult as they learn to use the questions as tools for opening the door to more and more questions about the problems they encounter. Teaching them to use questions as a means of identifying more questions to ask is teaching them a core element of critical thinking. The social-emotional learning that happens from the two rules will transfer to the cognitive skills students need in academic learning. Curiosity—Why did this happen? What could I have done differently? What is connected to what in this situation?—is a core cognitive skill. Providing modeling to help students develop curiosity is crucial during the middle school years.

In the conversations I have described in this chapter, each student reached a point where they made a statement that was evidence of social-emotional learning (see Figure 3.2). The most important thing about those statements is that students reached them on their own as

STUDENT'S STATEMENT	SKILL
I was part of the problem today.	Responsibility for actions
I did all of the things they are saying and I know how they saw it.	Perspective taking
I should have stopped to ask questions in my mind first.	Learning to think before acting
I did not make her feel safe or good.	Using the two rules to analyze a problem
Now that I am thinking about it, I get mad when I am not able to talk when I want to talk.	Learning to identify a problem
I think asking more questions and talking with someone else like an adult would be better before you do something.	Learning better ways to solve problems
I know what we need to do. We need to all get together and tell her we are sorry. We should not have done that to her. We need to give her a hug.	Empathy

Figure 3.2. *Skills students learned from the two rules*

part of their process of working through the situation that brought them to my office. I didn't sit down with them with the goal of pushing them to reach those moments. My goal was to support them as they worked through their own mental processing of their situations. I never knew for sure where that process would take them or how far they would get, but I knew that the two-rules culture of our school gave them firm ground for moving forward. The students' accomplishments in social-emotional learning were the result of their own work. As a result, they owned their accomplishments with pride and felt good about the changes they were making.

Finally, the two rules weren't a substitute for consequences laid out in the student handbook. We weren't a rogue school that used warm, fuzzy feelings as a substitute for discipline. However, when a student had a consequence from the handbook as a result of their actions, they understood *why* they had that consequence. They took responsibility for the action that led to the consequence and they had the emotional skills to understand how their actions affected other people. And they weren't labeled as "bad kids" when they had consequences. They were all learners who had the power to make different choices going forward. I often said that there were no bad kids, only bad choices.

I tried to avoid suspensions whenever I could by negotiating with the dean of students. If it was at all possible, I would ask for mandated sessions with the school counselor and sessions with me for two-rules conversations instead of a suspension. My philosophy was if a student could learn how to understand themselves better and choose different behaviors in the future, that was 100 percent better than having a suspension that might put them on a path toward dropping out of school and encounters with law enforcement. However, some behaviors that endangered other students guaranteed a suspension. I didn't negotiate in those situations. Keeping students safe was half of my promise to the entire school.

But even when students were suspended, I found ways to keep them connected to the school. Members of a church in our city who were retired teachers volunteered to provide this service. Students had the option of reporting to the church for a full school day. The volunteers came to the school to collect assignments and the resources suspended students would need, then mentored the students as they completed the work. Families provided transportation to and from the church.

Having just two rules sounds very simple, but it's actually quite complex. Those two rules are tools for helping students develop habits of mind that have the power to take them in a good direction. Students who learn to ask the two questions before taking action—Will this make me/them feel good? Will this make me/them feel safe?—are learning social skills, analytical skills, and questioning skills. They are learning how to take another person's perspective. They are learning to gather information when they face a problem so they can see the situation in the broadest possible perspective. They are learning to be people who think about the well-being of their community.

Resources

Nancy Frey, Douglas Fraser, and Dominique Smith, *All Learning Is Social and Emotional: Helping Students Develop Essential Skills for the Classroom and Beyond* (ASCD, 2019).

In the beginning of this book, the authors ask, "Does focusing on SEL take away from academics?" Their answer: "When students develop prosocial behaviors and self-regulation skills, they learn more; students with unaddressed problematic behavior learn less." Frey, Fraser, and Smith show educators many ways to integrate SEL into the curriculum, including examples of types of feedback that are more effective because they attend to social-emotional development. This book will help educators develop strategies for building students' self-efficacy about learning, helping students regulate their emotions, helping them develop cognitive skills linked to specific goals, and helping them develop social skills. The end of each chapter has boxed text that summarizes the takeaways from the chapter, and an appendix provides literary resources for social and emotional learning.

Thomas R. Hoerr, *Taking Social Emotional Learning Schoolwide: The Formative Five Skills for Students and Staff* (ASCD, 2020).

This book shows educators how to build five essential SEL skills—empathy, self-control, integrity, embracing diversity, and grit—into every aspect of a school's culture. Each chapter begins with a survey that shows readers how their school is performing on key elements of SEL. These include a "Vision, Mission, Values Survey," a "Practices Survey," a "People Survey," a "Narrative Survey," and a "Place Survey." The surveys are followed with a chapter that provides guidance and ideas for improving a school's culture related to SEL. Each chapter ends with questions designed to help readers think in concrete terms about how SEL is operating in their school.

Rebecca Roland, ***The Art of Talking with Children: The Simple Keys to Nurturing Kindness, Confidence, and Creativity in Kids*** (HarperOne, 2020).

Rebecca Roland is an oral and written language specialist in the neurology department of Boston Children's Hospital and a lecturer at Harvard University. In a YouTube presentation about this book, Roland called it a "translational project." She says, "It's designed to take what we know about conversations with kids from the research and translate it into something that's actionable, feasible, and fun for parents, teachers, and caregivers." *The Art of Talking with Children* introduces Roland's concept of rich talk with children, conversation that helps build relationships, develop learning skills, become more confident and independent, become more open to difference, learn play skills, and manage their temperament. Children who aren't exposed to rich talk struggle to connect with others and may have greater difficulty developing language skills. This book takes readers through eight domains of rich talk with children, showing through examples how adults can pick up on cues from children and open up conversations that help them explore important issues. This is a book for any adult who wants to understand what children are thinking and feeling and help them develop in ways that will prepare them for a life of rich connections with others. You can see Roland discuss the book in a YouTube presentation at https://www.youtube.com/watch?v=fjrqlITG0ow.

4

Building Resilience Based on Trust and Relationships

High childhood resilience is related to substantial reductions in lifetime mental illness.
—Welsh Adverse Childhood Experience (ACE) and Resilience Study

Recently a young, overwhelmed school principal said to me, "It seems like these days one of the biggest parts of a principal's job is being a therapist." It's no wonder this principal felt overwhelmed. In 2016, the National Survey of Children's Health found that 46 percent of children aged 17 or younger had experienced at least one trauma.[1] As people who see young people in their school five days a week, school principals see how adverse experiences affect students and many administrators struggle to find solutions for them.

In this chapter, I look at how relationships based on trust are the keystone of a positive school culture. More than that, trusting relationships with students are a pathway to healing and sometimes even survival for students who have experienced trauma. For many students in your building, trauma will not be a past experience. They will be in the midst of trauma that is with them every day. This chapter describes how we worked at our two-rules school to create relationships with students that helped them build resilience. We did this in a school where at least 75 percent of the students were living through trauma, most of which was caused by the impact of poverty on their families.

The Adverse Childhood Experiences Study

In 1998, a group of researchers and physicians who study preventive medicine published an article that reported on the findings of the first large study on the long-term physical effects of childhood trauma. The Adverse Childhood Experiences (ACEs) Study asked adults who were patients at a California clinic to complete a survey that asked questions about their traumatic experiences in childhood, their current state of health, and their current health-related behaviors. The survey asked participants if they had experienced sexual abuse, physical abuse, or psychological abuse before the age of 18. Other questions were designed to identify if respondents had grown up in a household in which someone was an alcoholic or drug abuser, if they had seen someone being violent toward their mother, if a member of the household was mentally ill, or if a member of the household had gone to prison.

The questionnaire also asked about participants' engagement with ten risk factors that are related to the leading causes of death and illness in the United States: "smoking, severe obesity, physical inactivity, depressed mood, suicide attempts, alcoholism, any drug abuse, parental drug abuse [injection with a needle], a high lifetime number of sexual partners ($\geq$ 50), and a history of having a sexually transmitted disease."[2] Finally, the study linked data from the survey questionnaires with medical histories the respondents provided. The researchers collected data on heart disease, cancer, stroke, chronic bronchitis or emphysema, and broken bones (which the study treated as a proxy for unintentional injuries).

This landmark study found that the prevalence of and risk of behaviors and conditions that affect health and even survival increased with the number of exposures to trauma respondents had experienced in childhood.[3] The study also found that respondents who had been exposed to four or more traumatic experiences in childhood were more likely to have sexually transmitted diseases (as a result of having a large number of sexual partners) and to be alcoholics or drug users.

The link between adult behavior and childhood trauma wasn't breakthrough information. Sociologists and psychologists had been publishing information about these links for a long time. What was new about the data in the ACEs study was the link between childhood trauma and poor physical health in adulthood. The data showed that adults who had adverse experiences in childhood were more likely to have heart disease, cancer, chronic lung disease, skeletal fractures, and liver disease in adulthood.[4] As this was the first study of its kind, the scope was limited to identifying the link between childhood trauma and adult health. The authors briefly discussed the things children might turn to (smoking, drinking, using drugs) as a way of coping with anger, depression, and anxiety. These behaviors are linked to many of the diseases the ACEs study linked to childhood trauma.

The ACEs study has been criticized for a number of reasons. Some critics feel that the fact that the survey relied on self-reporting is a weakness of the data. Others say that the study is framed in a way that tends to blame parents and caregivers for the adverse experiences of children instead of looking at the systemic causes of the poverty that creates stress within households. These critics point out that the study focused on "household dysfunction" without looking at the harms poverty brings, such as "food insecurity, unaffordable, and often inadequate, housing, societal marginalisation, decrease in living standards or inequality."[5] They point to a sharp rise in economic inequality in the United States since the 1980s and the large decline in families with middle-class incomes as a leading cause of adverse childhood experiences. Dimitri Hartas, a professor of education studies, argues that an effective response to ACEs should include prevention policies that increase resilience in children and their families.[6]

In 1998, the link between early trauma and adult health was poorly understood. The authors of the ACES study admitted that "comprehensive strategies are needed to identify and intervene with children and families who are at risk for these adverse experiences and their related outcomes."[7] We now know that not all children experiencing trauma turn to drugs or alcohol, although many do. In the twenty-first century, research has been done that looks at why some children cope with trauma better than others and what factors explain these differences.

Although there are reasons to critique the 1998 ACEs study, it provided a new framework for thinking about the possibility that childhood trauma can have a lifelong impact on a person's health. The research that has been done since then that built on those findings offers hope and important information about interventions that can be made *while a child is experiencing trauma* that can change the lifelong outcome for them. Teachers and administrators can't remove trauma from the lives of their students. But they can be trusted adults for those students: grownups who present the same stable temperament every day, who have predictable reactions to situations, who consistently interact with each student in a friendly and caring way, who help students solve daily problems, and who want the best for every student who walks through the door of their school.

Resilience Resources for Children

Resilience has emerged as a key factor in a child's ability to cope with adverse experiences. A recent study conducted by the National Health Service of Wales looked at the role of trusted adults in helping children develop resilience. This study used face-to-face interviews with 2,497 adults to look at the links between access to a trusted adult and having access to resources that build resilience in childhood.

The Welsh National Health Service study found that half of the adults in Wales had had four or more adverse experiences during childhood. However, adults who had the kind of support that builds resilience in childhood had a decreased risk of mental illness in adulthood. The health service asked 2,500 adults to rank their access to twelve resilience resources (Figure 4.1).

Figure 4.1. *The twelve childhood resilience resources*

1. I had people to look up to.

2. Getting an education was important to me.

3. My parents/caregivers knew a lot about me.

4. I tried to finish activities that I started.

5. I was able to solve problems without harming myself or others (e.g., without using drugs or being violent).

6. I knew where to go in my community to get help.

7. I felt I belonged in my school.

8. My family would stand by me during difficult times.

9. My friends would stand by me during difficult times.

10. I was treated fairly in my community.

11. I had opportunities to develop skills to help me succeeed in life (like job skills and skills to care for others).

12. I enjoyed my community's cultures and traditions.

Source: Karen Hughes, Kat Ford, Alisha R. Davies, Lucia Homolova, and Mark A. Bellis, *Sources of Resilience and Their Moderating Relationships with Harms from Adverse Childhood Experiences. Report 1: Mental Illness* (Wrexham: Public Health Wales, 2017).

Analysis of the data showed that people who had four or more adverse experiences in childhood and did not have access to a trusted adult also had low or no access to resilience resources. But people who had a similar number of adverse childhood experiences and *did* have access to a trusted adult were more likely to have access to social networks and community activities. The survey participants who had trusted adults in their lives scored high on seven key resilience resources when they were children: they had someone they could look up to, their parents or caregivers knew a lot about them, they felt like they belonged at school, they had supportive friends, help was available to them in the community, and they were culturally engaged with their community. The participants who had continuous access to a trusted adult were over five times more likely to develop skills that would serve them well in adulthood. The important findings from this study are first, that a trusted adult can be a bridge to resources that develop resilience in children even when a child is undergoing trauma, and second, that when children have access to those resources, they can develop skills that will prepare them for a successful adult life.[8]

As I looked at this list, what jumped out at me was that a two-rules school can be a place where students have access to many of those resources. Teaching students to ask, "Will this make me/them feel safe?" and "Will this help me/them feel good?" prepares them to be the kind of friend who will stand by a student undergoing difficulties (#8 in Figure 4.1). It creates an environment where students feel they belong at school (#7).

When a school principal and the teachers in the school model the two rules consistently when they interact with students, the school has a culture where students are treated fairly (#10) and where adults know their students because they have developed relationships with them (#3). Students know that there are people in the school they can turn to for help when they need it, and they aren't afraid to ask for it (# 6). When they struggle to complete a task, there will be an adult who can encourage them and support them (#4). There will be people in the school building that students look up to (#1). All of these resources put together provide a setting for a student to feel that their education is important for their future (#2).

A Trusted Adult Models Resilience Resources

This section discusses how a teacher students respected and liked modeled trustworthiness in a way that helped a class learn friendship skills that made them a resilience resource for a struggling student. The two-rules culture of our school helped students who engaged in group bullying learn the impact of what they had done and how to work to become trustworthy people.

Hunter was a student who had trouble fitting in. For one thing, he lived in a community that was far enough away from the school that he rode the bus. Houses were far apart in the rural area where he lived and there wasn't much of a chance for kids to get to know each other socially. In contrast, most of his classmates lived in neighborhoods near enough to the school to walk. Hunter had gone through elementary school in a different town, so he wasn't part of the network of students who lived near Fall Ridge Middle School. Another factor was that Hunter's home situation was very difficult. He lived in a household with extended family that included his grandparents, his mother, and his uncles. None of the men in the household were working; they didn't have the cognitive skills to get and keep a job.

It was clear to me that Hunter had had no opportunities to learn social skills. The adults in his household were not good examples and he wasn't able to learn them in peer groups because there weren't opportunities for kids to socialize in his rural location. Since coming to Fall Ridge, he had not found a successful way of making connections with his classmates. Hunter's way of coping with his high stress levels was to shut himself in his tiny bedroom (which was about the size of a half-bathroom) and play computer games. He was socially awkward and his attempts to connect with his classmates annoyed them.

We didn't know this at the time of the incident I'm about to describe, but he had begun cutting himself. He always wore long sleeves to conceal his scars. While we didn't know about the cutting, we knew that Hunter was in a traumatic situation, and we had already arranged for him to get support off campus at the nearby Center for Children's Services.

One day his teacher came to my office. Mr. Carter was very upset. He normally had a calm and steady personality. It took a lot to make him angry, but that day he was there. He told me that the entire class had said that Hunter had stolen an upcoming test from Mr. Carter's desk and shared it with other students in the class. When I talked to the students who had reported Hunter so I could gather information about the incident, I noticed that all of them were telling a nearly identical story. That was a red flag for me. I asked for a meeting with everyone involved—the class, including Hunter, and Mr. Carter.

I began the meeting with a recap of what I had been told. Then I paused. I said, "The entire class said that this is what happened." And I waited.

Gabrielle began to speak. "Mrs. Yoho, I guess I was the one that started this. At first, we thought it would be funny because Hunter is always doing things to us and it gets on our nerves. We did not mean for it to get this big."

"I see," I said. And I waited some more.

Tristan spoke up then and said that what they had done was wrong. "We all know better than this." Then Shelby said, "We were just trying to teach a lesson, I think."

"Okay, what was the lesson?" I asked. A long pause.

"Was this a lesson of trust?" I asked

Brooke spoke up. "It was a lesson not to trust any of us. We were not truthful. We lied about the situation. That is not being trustworthy.

Hunter should not trust us. We should all apologize to him and we should also apologize to Mr. Carter."

"You made some good suggestions, Brooke. However, it still does not answer the question of what lesson were all of you trying to teach Hunter by lying about him stealing the test."

Gabrielle said, "I guess it was not a lesson. We wanted to show him we were getting even with him for being mean to us. We wanted him to get in trouble because he is always mean to us. He smells and he bugs us."

"Oh, I see," I said. "It was not a lesson you were teaching. You were getting even with him. When you say teaching a lesson, that makes it his fault, not yours."

Then others begin to speak. "He does bug us. When I am trying to get in the door, he blocks my way." Another student said, "Yeah, when I want to get by him in the hall, he moves in front of me. His locker is next to mine, and when I am at my locker he doesn't give me any space to let me get to my stuff."

"I see," I said. I paused for a moment, then said, "Hunter is listening to all of this, I am listening, and so is Mr. Carter. I am thinking about all of the words and examples you have used. It seems there are a few things missing. Can any of you think what may be missing?"

Tristan spoke up first. "We did not think about asking Hunter."

"What would you ask Hunter?" I asked.

Tristan answered, "I think he is friends with a few people, but maybe he wasn't trying to bug us. Maybe he was just joking around with us, and we didn't understand it."

"Hunter, you have been quiet the whole time," I said. "Do you want to say anything?" Hunter said, "I don't really want to say anything. I am just listening."

I responded. "Okay, Hunter, that is fine." Then I addressed myself to the entire class. "I think there is a great deal of work we can all do together to understand this situation better and learn how to improve our approaches to each other. Mr. Carter, I think the social worker can come in one time per week to work with the group."

Students worked with the social worker on the lessons they could learn from their interactions. They looked at how they were treating each other and how they had worked together to bully an individual. Instead of standing up against bullying, they had banded together to validate reasons for their bullying actions. The social worker emphasized thinking about how the actions we do make others feel. The class learned about taking a moment to look at a situation before they acted so they could begin to see things from different points of view. We did exercises with them that asked them to put themselves in both positions in a situation so they could develop an appreciation of another person's perspective. For example, students explored both roles in a situation in a line in the cafeteria where one student conveyed to another with words or body language: "Don't get close to me in line. I don't want to be close to you." Putting themselves in both roles in this interaction helped the class develop empathy and insight.

Mr. Carter was a highly respected teacher and coach. The class felt horrible about what they had done and about the fact that they had broken trust with him. When he spoke to them in the meeting I had with the class, he talked about the trust they had built together as a class and as individuals. "Trust is something you earn and you never want to break," he said. "You have to work at gaining respect and trust. We will have to work hard at building our relationships together back up."

After this incident, Hunter became part of the intervention team at our school. (See Chapter 6 for more about intervention teams.) We also established a regular time for him to go to counseling at the Center for Children's Services. In addition, I met with him weekly and he worked with the social worker in the building. Mr. Carter began working with him as a mentor. He pulled in some of the other kids in their sessions so they could all work on friendship skills. School staff also made home visits to try to work on the situation at home.

The two-rules culture in our school prepared the students who had participated in the group bullying to understand how they had broken trust—with Hunter, with Mr. Carter, and even with themselves. We were a school whose mantra was "You can be part of the solution or you can be part of the problem," and they had caused a problem that affected a lot of people. In the meeting I had with the class, the students began to look at Hunter's behavior from his perspective. They took responsibility for their actions. They expressed remorse and they truly understood the gravity of the situation. They realized that broken trust means broken relationships. With support and mentoring, Hunter and his classmates learned about different types of friendships and Hunter began to make some friends. He stayed in school and graduated.

In that meeting, I listened carefully to what the students had to say and let them know that I was hearing them. But I didn't accept easy answers from them. I never let them off the hook. I pushed them to look deeper at the meaning of their words, to examine the biases in the language they used even as they were coming to terms with what they had done. That meeting wouldn't have been as productive as it was if the students weren't immersed in the culture of the two rules. No one had to say what those rules were at that meeting. Everyone knew that what they had done didn't make Hunter feel good and didn't make him feel safe. They knew that they didn't feel good about what they had done and they were ready to take responsibility for their actions and learn how to do better. The two-rules culture of our school created the environment that made that meeting possible.

Our response to this incident helped students in Mr. Carter's class develop several resilience resources. They learned how to create bridges to friendship for a person who was new to their group. In that process, they became a resilience resource for Hunter. They learned the importance of being trustworthy, a skill that would serve them well in adulthood. They learned that what seemed like a small action to them was group bullying that could cause harm. They learned to pause and reflect before taking action. Each of these lessons was supported by the two questions of the two rules.

Trusted Adults at School

Identifying People Who Are Trusted Adults in Your School

Brooklyn Raney, the author of *One Trusted Adult: How to Build Strong Connections & Healthy Boundaries with Young People,* writes, "Having [a trusted adult] in your life when you are young can significantly reduce risk, give you a safe place for processing normal life questions, provide a teacher and model important life skills, and help you calibrate your inner compass. . . . Being there for young people, just being there, is a small ask that yields great gains."[9]

Who are the trusted adults in your building? Students will quickly identify which adults they can trust. Any adult who is consistently present, who conveys to students that they are on their side and want to hear from them, who welcomes interactions with them, and who maintains clear and healthy boundaries during those interactions will become a trusted adult. The school custodian may be someone the students trust and respect. At Fall Ridge, our school resource officer was a trusted adult and a friend to many students. He used a community policing approach to his job; he wanted to build relationships with students so he could work with them to prevent crime and help them make good decisions.[10] The door to his office was always open. Students would drop in to talk to him before classes started and during their lunch hour. They knew he was on their side, and he helped them solve many problems, both small and large.

It's just as important to notice when someone in your building who should be a trusted adult is someone students are avoiding. A social worker who isn't someone students trust will be a hindrance instead of a help in a two-rules school. It's your responsibility as principal to find out what the reason is. Is the social worker burned out? Is their workload too heavy? Do they feel undervalued? Can you offer support that will ease the situation for them? Find out as best you can why students are reluctant to work with a professional in your building who should be a trusted adult for them. If a situation has been mishandled and that has

Figure 4.2. *Characteristics of a trusted adult at school*

Exhibits steady, predictable behavior every day

Sets good boundaries
- No social media relationship with students
- No texting with students
- Limits out-of-school relationships to public, structured settings (e.g., church, athletic events)

Always keeps promises

Doesn't discuss other students

Makes it clear to students that they want the best possible future for them

Connects students with resources they need

Shows students paths to self-efficacy

Celebrates each accomplishment a student makes on their way to reaching a goal

Follows all school policies (i.e., doesn't make up their own rules that go against school policies)

Source: Brooklyn Raney, *One Trusted Adult: How to Build Strong Connections & Healthy Boundaries with Young People* (Circle Talk Publishing, 2019).

compromised a professional's ability to work with students, find a way that respects the viewpoint of everyone involved to repair that person's relationship with students.

Identifying Teacher Bias toward Students

After the meeting I had with Mr. Carter's class, he and I discussed what had happened. He was amazed that I knew right away that the students had lied. He could not believe he had been fooled like that.

I told him, "In situations like the one you faced, it is important to calmly step back and look at the situation without biases. You were looking with a biased lens. You prejudged everyone involved based on your beliefs. You believed that the rest of the class were good people who weren't likely to do something wrong. And you believed that Hunter was likely to do something wrong."

After a long pause he finally looked at me and said, "I think you are right."

I always told my staff that when you are going to make a decision that results in a disciplinary action, gather all of the facts before you react. Calmly look at the entire picture. The picture I was seeing did not line up. I know all of these children, and I knew that they never agreed as a group about anything!

This points out the importance of relationships with students. I knew how those students felt about many things, I knew how they interacted with each other, and I knew about their home lives. That information was invaluable as I approached the situation Mr. Carter brought to me. I emphasized relationships with students to my staff, mostly by example. Recently, one of my teachers recalled:

One of the most significant changes that occurred when Mrs. Yoho came to our school was the interaction between teachers and students. One of the strategies that Mrs. Yoho brought . . . was the "nurtured heart" approach. Through this strategy, teachers were encouraged to say positive things to students during class and to praise students who were following expectations. [Through] this approach . . .teachers were able to build positive relationships with students. Mrs. Yoho was the first principal I had that stressed the importance of relationships with students. [That] was one of the most important aspects of building a positive . . . culture at our school.

Teachers who consistently interact with students in this way become adults kids can trust. And teachers who choose not to do this put up a wall that can make their job very difficult. Rita Pierson, a much-admired educator who taught for four decades, spoke about this in a Ted Talk. She said, "A colleague said to me one time, 'They don't pay me to like the kids. They pay me to teach a lesson. They should learn it, I should teach it, case closed.' I said to her, 'You know, kids don't learn from people they don't like.' She said, 'That's just a bunch of hooey.' And I said, 'Well, your year is going to be long and arduous.' And it was."[11]

Before teachers can build authentic relationships with students, they need to uncover their biases, just as Mr. Carter did. When I first came to Fall Ridge, I wanted to work with my staff to understand what the true culture of our building was. My administrative intern and I designed an exercise for the staff to really dig into that issue. In one of our first professional learning days, we met each staff member at the door to the meeting room and handed them a colored piece of construction paper. The color told them which table they were assigned to.

On their tables, they found construction paper, chart paper, yarn, tape, markers, colored pencils, stickers, crayons, old magazines, old pieces of fabric, and other assorted craft materials. Once they were all seated, I said, "At your table, you have art supplies and a large piece of chart paper to create a picture of a student in our school. We are asking each table to create a depiction of student you see in the building. What do they look like? What is your student's name? Tell us about their background. What about their learning? Behavior? You have 15 minutes."

When the staff had completed their depictions of students, we asked them to hang them around the room. One teacher interrupted us before we even started talking about what the depictions conveyed and said: "All of these students have negative images." I said, "So what does that tell us as a staff?" They answered, "We see kids negatively."

That started a discussion. Now we were at the core of the culture. They had a negative approach to the students and we needed to dig in to shift this mindset. We would not be able to accomplish any goals until we were able to change this culture so that we truly believed that all of our students could learn and we valued them as individuals. We also needed to understand their families.

In her book *The Power of Our Words: Teacher Language That Helps Children Learn,* Paula Denton writes, "What we say to others can deeply affect their sense of who they are and who they might become." She talks about the importance of using direct and authentic words when speaking with students. This kind of language "allows children to feel respected and to know clearly what the teacher means." I used this book as the basis for professional development for the teachers in my building. Here are some examples from Denton's book that illustrate the nurturing approach I encouraged teachers to use when they spoke to students:

- I like the way you are having consideration for others.

- I really appreciate how you are planning well. You are being very organized.

- You are showing a real talent for this assignment in the way you are putting all these pieces of information together.

- Thank you for contributing to the happy mood in our classroom right now.

- You are being marvelous in how you are showing perseverance.

- I appreciate how you are handling your strong feelings very well.

- I like how you're choosing what's important. That shows excellent judgment.

Source: Paula Denton, *The Power of Our Words: Teacher Language That Helps Children Learn* (Northeast Foundation for Children, 2014), 4, 13, 83.

Creating a Staff of Trusted Adults

When your school's culture is based on trusting relationships, students will feel safe enough to come to you when they feel something is not right. They may not know the reason why they feel uncomfortable, but they will know when they don't feel good or safe. And they will come and ask you for help. When that happens, you will know that your efforts to support their mental health are working. And you will have a deep responsibility to listen to them and address their concerns in a way that respects both the students and the staff member involved.

I've mentioned several times that Fall Ridge had a high percentage of Black students in the district as a result of a so-called urban renewal project in a city several hours away. The housing projects and neighborhoods where these students had been born and had lived all their lives had been demolished to make way for a major city project and the families were relocated. A good share of those families had come to our county several years before I became the principal at Fall Ridge.

I worked to create an environment that normalized Black culture in our school. When we had community members come to our school, we always included leaders from the Black community. When we read books for Drop Everything and Read Day (see Chapter 2), we used books by Black authors about Black kids the same age as our students. I visited the families of Black students to make sure their children had what they needed to do well in school. I encouraged Black students to take leadership roles, for example on the Student Advisory Board (see Chapter 6). I encouraged Black students to apply for scholarships and grants. *All* of the students at Fall Ridge knew that the two rules were for them. They knew what to expect from the promise part of those rules: they expected to feel good and feel safe at school.

One day a group of students came to my office. They told me that they believed their teacher was racist and said that they didn't feel good when they were in her class. I asked them what was happening in the class to make them feel this way. They said that she always called on the same kids and that she sent more Black kids to the office for discipline.

I always relied on data when possible, so I told the students that I would review the data on disciplinary incidents for this teacher for the past three months and would get back to them. I also said that I would talk to other students in the teacher's classes to see what their impressions were about what was happening in the classroom. I did this unobtrusively, of course. I called individual students in over time and talked to them in a way that didn't make it apparent that I was focused on a particular teacher. When I looked at the data, it showed that their teacher in fact had a lower rate of sending Black kids for discipline than other teachers in the building. I called the students back to give them my report.

I heard from the other students in Mrs. Jackson's classes that they didn't perceive a problem. I knew students often perceived the same thing through different eyes because of life experiences. Their perceptions were their perceptions. How to make them feel good in Mrs. Jackson's class was the most important issue to figure out.

I showed them the data. I didn't use it to prove them wrong. I used it to show them what the numbers were saying about the issue of discipline. I said, "Now this data on discipline is only part of the picture. You also told me that you feel that Mrs. Jackson is calling on the same students and not Black students. I think that Mrs. Jackson would feel very sad if she heard this and would want to do anything she could to make you feel good in her class. Do you think you would feel comfortable talking to her if I was in the meeting with you?" The students immediately rejected this option. Because their trust with Mrs. Jackson was compromised, they were afraid that talking with her would have bad consequences for them. Even though I knew that Mrs. Jackson would be very open to hearing what they had to say, I wasn't surprised that they didn't feel that talking with her openly was a good idea for them. I respected their decision and told them that I would talk with Mrs. Jackson and would report back to them about that conversation. I assured them that Mrs. Jackson would never know the names of the students who had come to me. The students were visibly relieved to hear this. They wouldn't have to speak face to face with their teacher, Mrs. Jackson wouldn't know their identities, and I wasn't giving up on their problem. We didn't have a solution that was good for them yet.

The next step was to talk with Mrs. Jackson. I spoke with her in a way that showed support for her but didn't shy away from the issue. I said that some students had come to me and said that they felt she was showing favoritism. "Some students are feeling that your actions make them feel like you favor certain students. Can we do some reflection together about what specific actions in your classroom might be making them feel this way?" Mrs. Jackson was stunned and struggled to think what she might be doing that gave students this impression. Again, I felt that it was important to gather data instead of addressing this issue by responding emotionally. This may well have been a case of unconscious racial bias. I was aware of that. But I also knew from my teaching days that another kind of bias may have been at work. When I was a teacher, a principal had pointed out to me that teachers sometimes unconsciously call on students in the side of the room that corresponds to their handedness. If they are right-handed, without realizing it, they call on students sitting to their right. And if they are left-handed, they call on students to their left. I knew from the seating chart for Mrs. Jackson's classroom that all of the Black students sat on the same side of the room. We needed data.

I suggested that Mrs. Jackson use one of the school's video recorders to record a teaching session so she could play it back and watch herself. I gave her several suggestions to make sure that she called on every student. One was that she make a list of the names of students in her class and check off the names of the students she called on immediately after class as another way of collecting data. (When I was teaching, I had a piece of poster board with students' names along the right and left edges. Each name had a small clothespin next to it. As I called on a student, I would remove the clothespin and put it in the basket. That way, I was making sure in real time that each student was called on. It was very low-tech, but it worked.)

I also asked Mrs. Jackson to think about what she could do to make each student feel better in her classroom. For example, she could greet each student at the door by name and make it clear that she was glad to see them. I said I would check back with her in a week to see how things were going.

Then I called the students back in and told them I had met with Mrs. Jackson and that we had talked about improvements she could make in her classroom. The students thanked me for my efforts and said "Mrs. Yoho, we knew that you would want to know about this issue." That validated so much of what I was trying to accomplish at Fall Ridge. Every student felt that they had a right to feel good at school. And if they didn't feel good, they knew that I wanted to rectify the problem.

Mrs. Jackson was very invested in solving this issue. She happened to be left-handed, and what the video showed was that she was unconsciously calling on students to her left more often than those on her right. And the Black students were sitting on her right.

This incident galvanized her to work harder to be an adult all of her students could trust. She began attending school dances and other events students were involved in. She grew closer to all of her students and ended up having a much better year than she had imagined she could.

The students who had come to me saw that Mrs. Jackson was working to correct how she conducted herself in the classroom. They began to trust her.

There are several things to note about this issue. First, nobody got defensive when the students raise the issue of racism in the classroom. Instead, the adults involved were focused on how that impression was created so they could correct those behaviors. I honored their feelings in my conversations with them. People's feelings are their feelings. When our intentions don't yield the reactions we think they will, that is not the problem of the person who is reacting in a way that surprises us. Actions, not intentions, are what count. As educators, it is our responsibility to act in ways that students can rely on. They need to know that they can trust us not to act in ways that will hurt them.

Second, I worked with Mrs. Jackson in a way that respected her. Both of us trusted each other because we both had the students' welfare as our top priority. I had made a promise to students that everyone would feel good and safe in our school. We needed to figure out how to make that promise a reality for the students who had come to me. Equally important was Mrs. Jackson's right to feel good and feel safe. I spoke with her in a way that showed my confidence in her and in her ability to make adjustments that would solve the problem. Approaching the issue as a problem that required more data gave her space to see for herself what specific actions she could correct. This is a good way to build up staff members so they can become adults all of their students can trust.

Third, I was transparent with the students about the process I was using. I told them what my plan was and reported what I had learned at several points in the process. And I didn't stop until they felt comfortable in Mrs. Jackson's class. The students had come to me because they trusted me and it was very important to maintain that trust.

When you are working to create a staff of trusted adults, you may need to provide targeted support to encourage a teacher who is learning to shift their approach. One of the faculty at Fall Ridge had been teaching for many years. He was old school in his interactions with students. He was a great storyteller in the classroom and many students liked him. But he didn't respond well when students didn't follow the rules. He liked kids who were rule followers.

I put a student in his class who I knew he could help. Jasmine had been held back in elementary school, so she was taller than her sixth-grade classmates. She had been through a lot, and by the time she got to Fall Ridge she had put up walls that were all sharp edges. She was a very injured person. But I knew both Jasmine and Mr. Stewart and I believed they could work well together. Each of them had traits that complemented the other person.

At first, Mr. Stewart began calling me to his classroom when Jasmine wasn't cooperating. This happened on a fairly regular basis for a while. I talked individually with both Jasmine and Mr. Stewart. I reminded him that kind words had great power and that he could do a lot for Jasmine by encouraging her and reinforcing her accomplishments. I said that I felt that he was uniquely qualified to bring out qualities in Jasmine that I had seen. I talked several times with Jasmine when I saw her in the lunchroom. I told her that I had put her in Mr. Stewart's classroom because I thought they could make a great team. Each of them had qualities that could complement each other, I said. Soon Mr. Stewart was bragging to me about Jasmine. They had bonded, and Mr. Stewart was using every positive resource to build Jasmine up. He had begun to see in her what I had seen—that she had the potential to become a leader. He showed her that she didn't need to use oppositional behavior as a defense, that there was another path she could use that would take her to a new place. Thanks in part to the encouragement Jasmine received from Mr. Stewart, she graduated from high school.

Sometimes a teacher needs support and encouragement as they work to expand their roles with their students. I gave Mr. Stewart a challenge and then supported him while he figured out a way to meet it. I kept a close eye on the situation and dropped encouraging words on both Jasmine and Mr. Stewart as they found a way to work together.

As a principal, you can do a lot to support teachers as they build skills in and out of the classroom that will help them become trusted adults for all of their students. You can encourage and support them as they find their own ways through challenges in their classrooms. You can provide professional development that will introduce them to new ways of speaking with students. You can update policies about boundaries as new technology creates new situations for teachers. You can remind them that you believe in them and appreciate the skills and talents they bring to your building. You can listen when they are struggling. Most important, by modeling what a trusted adult is for students *and* for your staff, your behavior will show them what your school needs from them.

Resilience Resource Inventory

The table below lists the twelve factors the adults in the Welsh National Health Service survey identified as resources that helped them survive traumas in their childhood. What resources does your school provide in each of these twelve areas? What programs or activities or policies could you add that would increase the resilience resources your school provides?

Resilience Resources for Students	Current Practices/ Programs	Ideas for Additional Supports
I had people I looked up to.		
Getting an education was important to me.		
My parents/caregivers knew a lot about me.		
I tried to finish activities that I started.		
I was able to solve problems without harming myself or others.		
I knew where to go in my community to get help.		
I felt I belonged in my school.		
My family would stand by me during difficult times.		
My friends would stand by me during difficult times.		
I was treated fairly in my community.		
I had opportunities to develop skills to help me succeed in life (like job skills and skills to care for others).		
I enjoyed my community's cultures and traditions.		

Resource List

Mike M. Milstein and Doris Annie Henry, *Leadership for Resilient Schools and Communities,* **2nd ed. (Corwin, 2008).**

This interactive book takes principals through the steps of building a school culture that teaches resilience skills to students. Chapter 1 includes exercises that show readers what their own level of resilience skills is and introduces the concept of the resilience wheel—a model that includes six elements of resilience resources. Chapter 2 focuses on building resilient communities and includes actions school administrators can take. Chapter 3 looks at specific ways to increase student resilience and nurture students' protective factors. Chapter 4, "Nurturing the Nurturers," is about increasing the resilience of staff, including removing school-based barriers to teacher resilience. Other chapters address increasing the resilience of the school, developing partnerships in the community that support resilience, and strategies for leading resilience.

Brooklyn L. Raney, *One Trusted Adult: How to Build Strong Connections and Healthy Boundaries with Young People* **(Brooklyn Raney LLC, 2019).**

This book should be required reading for everyone who interacts with adolescents. Most people think they know instinctively how to be trustworthy adults for young people, but this book shows through many real-life examples how seemingly innocuous actions can break trust with kids and cause harm. In a chapter on boundaries, Raney writes, "The world is constantly changing, teens are constantly changing, and we need to keep up. . . . There is no reason we should not continue practicing our skills in this area and discuss how we might handle specific situations." *One Trusted Adult* has three sections: Building Trust, Establishing Boundaries, and Creating Culture. The chapters are easy to process because they are based on stories from Raney's experiences as a mother and a school administrator. An appendix, "Summary of Tactics for Building Trust, Establishing Boundaries, and Creating Culture," offers many specific behaviors trusted adults should model.

Victoria E. Romero, Ricky Robertson, and Amber Warner, *Building Resilience in Children Impacted by Adverse Life Experiences: A Whole Staff Approach* **(Corwin, 2018).**

This book is primarily for teachers. It discusses the new normal teachers face in their classrooms: a higher proportion of families affected by poverty and the impact of technological change on how children behave. The thesis of the book is that people who interact with traumatized students can flip how they see disruptive behavior, bullying, or withdrawal. When school staff members look at these behaviors as forms of communication that are caused by things beyond a student's control, a door opens to teach new forms of communication. The book takes a schoolwide approach; it shows how every adult who works in a school, from bus drivers and cafeteria workers to nurses, social workers, and psychologists, can work together to develop what the authors call transformationist actions—responses to trauma-related behavior that help students learn new ways of communicating. Romero and her coauthors outline the specific behaviors students in rural, suburban, and urban schools are likely to exhibit when they are experiencing trauma and discuss the topics of suicidal ideation, bullying, and drug use. One of the many strengths of the book is its look at the characteristics of white teachers who helped Black students in urban, high-poverty schools close the achievement gap.

Horacio Sanchez, *The Poverty Problem: How Education Can Promote Resilience and Counter Poverty's Impact on Brain Development and Functioning* (Corwin, 2021).

This book looks at the impact of poverty on students through the lens of neuroscience. Sanchez notes that poverty impacts the development of the prefrontal cortex, compromising students' ability to focus, plan, and analyze. Poverty also diminishes language development, acting as "a gag on the voices of the poor." In response to this disheartening news, Sanchez presents principles of good instruction that have been successful with students of low socioeconomic status around the world. These practices are backed by neuroscience. Sanchez reports that resiliency research has found only one academic protective factor for brain development: reading. He writes "If reading lags, the brain begins to produce alternative pathways to compensate for brain regions not performing efficiently." These pathways become difficult to correct as children age. However, if even a struggling reader can maintain grade level, the structure and functioning of many regions of the brain will improve. A final chapter presents a plan for building resiliency resources at school.

5

Supporting Teachers and Students through Trauma

For every child who has experienced post-traumatic stress,
there are some who have experienced post-traumatic growth; the ability
to grow and excel because of their trauma, not despite it.
—Michael S. Gaskell, *Leading Schools through Trauma*

When your school has a two-rules culture, a foundation has been laid to support students and faculty through crises and trauma. That is because the two rules do more than help students learn empathy and how to ask questions to prevent them from responding reactively. The two-rules questions help students identify and articulate their feelings when something in their environment changes.

Supporting Individual Students through Trauma

When You Know about the Trauma

Sometimes the trauma a student has suffered is knowable. They will probably have an IEP based on a learning difference, an illness, or an injury. Providing the accommodations that student needs is an important part of serving them, but in a two-rules school, what can a principal do that goes beyond that? How can a principal make sure that a student experiencing trauma feels included and welcomed? And how can the two rules support those students?

One student at Fall Ridge experienced a traumatic brain injury at the age of four. He had outbursts every day. He couldn't tolerate pressure and would flee from his classroom. He was struggling hard and didn't know how to handle his situation. His teacher was trying to figure out how to help him, but she was struggling too. Each time he fled from his classroom, I would get the call to come help. Gradually, he was able to tell me that he didn't feel good or safe in his classroom and that that was why he was running away.

That was a good starting point. I asked him what would make him feel good and safe. He asked me to explain more about his injury to his classmates so they could understand what he was experiencing. And I worked with him on building up his tolerance to pressure bit by bit. By that time, I also had a brain injury and knew exactly how it felt to not be able to do things that the people around me could do with ease. Together, he and I learned what his specific triggers were. I talked with him about building up his strength—not physical strength, but brain strength. I told him it was a very hard thing to do but I believed he could do it. He learned what specific things he needed to work on and began building up his capacity to cope with triggers bit by bit, day by day, just like an athlete would build up physical strength.

We rearranged his schedule so he would have space to decompress between classes. And I encouraged him every day. Each day his tolerance for stress got just a bit longer. He was able to stay in school every day.

There were elements of this situation that were unique. My injury was similar in some ways to his, so I understood something about what daily life was like for him. But I approached his difficulty the way I would for any student at Fall Ridge. I made it clear to him that I wanted to know what he was feeling and what he was thinking. I wanted to know what the world looked like through his eyes. I wanted to know what would make him feel good. I wanted to know what would make him feel safe. I wanted to know what I could do to support him so he could reach the goal of staying in school. And he trusted me enough to tell me the answers to those questions.

When the Trauma Can't Be Spoken

Sometimes there are reasons a student can't say out loud what they are going through. For example, Whitney, the student I journaled with every day, couldn't tell me that she was having suicidal ideation in response to medical abuse at the hands of her mentally ill mother. She knew that that would have set in motion a plan to remove her from her home, but she needed to stay in the household to protect her younger brother as best she could. That was her goal.

In the face of trauma, students often grapple with the challenge of articulating their emotions and experiences. They may find themselves at a loss for words as they navigate the complexities of their personal trauma. Questions about their identity and the search for meaning further add to their struggles. Additionally, they may be uncertain and what constitutes normal reactions and what falls outside the realm of typical responses. Finding the language to express these deep-seated emotions and seeking clarity amidst confusion can be a significant part of their healing journey.

In such cases, art can provide an outlet that supports a student through some of the most challenging years of their development. We were fortunate at Fall Ridge to have access to I Sing the Body Electric, an art-based health initiative for students sponsored by a local medical facility. The name draws on the title of a poem in Walt Whitman's 1855 collection *Leaves of Grass*. The program was introduced to schools in seven districts in our region in all-school assemblies that explained that student participants could use art to explore any health concern they chose. Students worked with interns from local colleges who had expertise in a broad range of disciplines to develop their art projects.[1]

They chose themes related to drinking and driving, body image, drug use, AIDS, STDs, sexuality, suicide, depression, dating abuse, cutting, and other issues.[2] Many students chose issues related to mental health.

Becky, one of our Fall Ridge students, wanted to express a Goth identity but was getting flack from her family. She was always contrasted unfavorably with her ultra-feminine cousin, which frustrated her. She didn't want to look like her cousin. Becky was very intelligent, but the stress of her identity struggle was leading her toward trouble. She began having problems at home. Then her parents divorced. At that point, Becky became depressed. I began talking to her one-on-one and learned that she liked art. She was a perfect match for I Sing the Body Electric. I knew the coordinator of the program and arranged for it to come to our school. Becky was very excited about creating something for the program but wasn't sure what theme to use.

I talked to her about feeling good and feeling safe. When I asked her what feeling good meant to her, she responded, "I want to look in the mirror and be comfortable with what I see. I want to feel comfortable at school and not worry that people are looking at me and seeing something I am not." I pointed out that the mirror image could be a powerful one for her art and that it was directly related to the idea of safety. Becky responded, "Yes, I want to feel safe with who I am and feel that no one is judging me."

Becky remembers her experience with this art program to this day. She learned about herself through participating and saw that many students who created art for the program were also struggling. She saw that people responded to her art positively and that art was a way to communicate safely about her feelings. She says, "It is not always comfortable to have difficult conversations, but this made space for it. It turned things around for so many of us."

Art, music, theater, and creative writing are all ways for students to express what cannot be said in face-to-face conversations. Some students have a talent for creating comics. Work with students undergoing trauma to help them find a way to explore feelings and find community.

Supporting a School After a Trauma

A Foundation of Empathy Supports Everyone during a Crisis

The social and emotional skills the two rules teach provide a strong foundation for helping a school during or after a crisis or a traumatic event. Perhaps the best illustration I have of how the two-rules culture can support a school after a trauma is what happened at Fall Ridge after I was in a car accident that caused serious injury to my face and my brain. The staff met to discuss how they would break the news of my accident to the students. After students were informed, staff kept a close eye on them to monitor their emotions. I was a trusted adult for all of the students. They were used to seeing me first thing in the morning, in the lunchroom, in the hallways during the day, and at the end of the day when they left the school campus. My presence was a significant part of the structure of their days. The abrupt absence of a trusted adult for an indefinite time was traumatic for all of the Fall Ridge students. They weren't even sure if they would see me again at school.

The way the students responded was beautiful. A teacher later told me about what happened during this period. He said that students became more caring and empathetic with each other. They drew on my mantra question, the one that each student knew in their bones because they heard it every morning during announcements: do you want to be part of the problem or do you want to be part of the solution? The problem was clear. Would the school continue to operate the way it did when I was there or would they abandon the two rules and "let things go to the wolves," as the teacher phrased it? The students chose to be part of the solution, a decision that "really showed during this period," the teacher said. Their behavior at school actually improved significantly.

The staff responded by drawing even closer to the students and talking more often with them about their emotions. The teacher who has told me about this time said that "the staff was very fatherly and motherly to the students and guided them in the right directions." Everyone worked together to ensure that the school year was a success. The teacher said, "We all worked on a solution and stuck with it until Mrs. Yoho's return."

This incident could have gone the other way very easily. I had close, supportive relationships with the students. My sudden absence could have changed their equilibrium enough to undo much of the hard work we had done together. But the students had a good foundation based on the empathy they had developed for each other and on their close relationships with teachers who were trusted adults. And they cared about their school. We had gone from a school that the community saw as the worst in the district to a school they were proud of, a school that was a safe place. Fall Ridge was a haven for many students who lived with daily trauma in their homes and neighborhoods and they were eager to preserve that resource.

When a Student Dies

The death of a student is one of the hardest things for a school to process, whether the death is the result of an accident, an illness, or a student's decision to stop living. For many students, this may be their first encounter with death. This may be the first time they will be processing thoughts about mortality. Sadly, other students will already have encountered death, perhaps multiple times.

I guided Fall Ridge through the death of a student more times than I ever imagined I would. Poverty created circumstances that put our students in lethal danger. One especially tragic case provides a good illustration of how the two rules can support both a whole school and individual students in the aftermath of a student death.

The incident began when the Department of Children and Family Services removed twin sixth-grade boys, Dalton and Dillon, from their home and placed them in different foster homes. Although they were both removed, only Dillon had been deemed to be in danger at home. This was very traumatic for the brothers. Their only thought was how they could be reunited. Their sixteen-year-old sister talked with them every day to provide support and reassure them that the situation was temporary. But the circumstances were confusing and intolerable for Dalton, who had not been removed for neglect. He had been placed in a foster home 30 miles from his family without a reason that made sense to him. He wondered why he had been separated from his brother. As the days passed, he grew more and more upset.

The solution Dalton came up with was that of an impulsive preteen. He ran away after one week. He was quickly found and taken to a hospital for a medical evaluation. During that evaluation, he slipped away from the social worker who was with him, stole a pickup truck about a block from the hospital, and began driving on the highway toward his hometown. At some point, the twins' best friend, Chad, joined him and they continued on their quest to pick up Dillon. About six miles from their hometown, the road switched from macadam to gravel and Dalton lost control of the truck. It rolled over and ejected both boys.

Dalton died at the hospital the emergency crew took the boys to. Chad suffered serious injuries. He was a paraplegic after the accident and never spoke again. He died four years later.

I knew this would be a complex trauma for our students to process. But I also knew that the two rules could be a good support to them in the coming weeks. Here is what I said in the all-school assembly we had the day after the tragedy:

Good morning.

I know many of you listen to the news and to the radio and probably have heard the news already. Yesterday, we lost one of our students, Dalton Conklin, in a car accident. Also, we have one of our students in the hospital with very severe injuries who is fighting for his life right now.

Many of you may be friends with the boys and all of us are a family. So we are grieving today. It is okay to grieve. We will have many different emotions today.

Today at our school are many more people to help Ms. L. and Mrs. M. if you need to talk to someone. You also have OT [our school resource officer] and Mrs. F. They are always available.

Here are a couple of things I am going to try to think about today and tomorrow.

I am going to think about how it would be if I was a twin brother like Dillon trying to come back to school here. It would be pretty hard if everyone was talking about what happened, asking me questions, and telling me how sorry they were.

I would also get really sad if someone called me my brother's name, even if it was by accident.

So for today and tomorrow if you have questions ask the adults who are here to help. If you want to express your feelings to Dillon, let's work on how we can help him feel good and feel safe about being here. Can we make him some cards to deliver to him? When we find out about the funeral service for his brother, can we send something to the family? Let's talk and think about our two rules of feeling good and feeling safe so we can help Dillon come back to school.

The circumstances that led to Dalton's death were confusing for students who were not familiar with the protective services the Department of Children and Family Services provided to children. Staff worked to explain that piece of the situation to them. That was challenging to do without revealing private information, so the staff and I worked together to determine a good way to guide those conversations. Then students had to process the next layer, the fact that Dalton had not made a good or safe choice. This was difficult for them to do in the wake of Dalton's death. We talked a lot over the next weeks about safety and why rules are in place to make sure students are safe.

The staff and I worked together to form a sort of template for discussions with students about their feelings about this tragedy. Our intervention teams worked with students who wanted to know what they should do. We had a general script that staff used and adjusted as conversations developed. It began with a teacher or staff member saying, "Mrs. Yoho said in the assembly that when Dillon comes back, we want to make him feel good. We also want to make sure you're feeling good. What are you thinking about?" I instructed staff to wait for the student to speak. I reminded them that students need time to identify thoughts and feelings and then put them into words. I told the staff, "Wait time is think time. Let the kids think before you start telling." We already had a culture in our school where students were used to talking about feelings and knew they could trust adults in the building to hear them. Neither the staff nor the students were uncomfortable having this kind of conversation. The students came up with a good list of things they could do to support Dillon and to support each other in the coming weeks.

The student who suffered the most, of course, was Dillon, Dalton's twin. It was because of the neglect he was suffering at home that the twins had been put in foster care. Perhaps if he had just kept quiet his brother would still be alive. And every time he looked in the mirror, he saw his brother's face. Another thing that was difficult for Dillon was that the identity the twins had created was one of strength. They did not want to show any weakness. But Dillon was suffering immensely and did not feel strong. We later learned that Dalton had somehow contacted him after he stole the truck and said that he was coming to get him. But Dillon had refused to join his brother in a stolen vehicle because he knew that wasn't a safe choice, and he was wracked with guilt about that decision. It intensified his survivor's guilt.

Dillon wasn't able to trust the adults in his family. His trust with them had been broken. I was the main trusted adult for him during the weeks after his brother's death, and I worked with him one-on-one in my office to support him and help him refocus and rebuild. One day as we sat next to each other in my office, his whole body began shaking. His façade of strength crumbled and he howled his grief. I knew that this depth of emotion required the assistance of professionals and hit the call button for the school psychologist and school social worker. While we waited for them to arrive, I did what I could to be a calming presence for Dillon. With the support I and those two professionals provided for Dillon, he was able to process the first wave of his grief.

This story illustrates how the two rules can support a school through trauma at several levels. First, the two questions about feeling good and feeling safe help students understand and cope with their feelings after a sudden trauma. Those two questions—Are you feeling good? and Are you feeling safe?—are great door-openers in conversations with students. They lead to follow-up questions that guide students through the process of naming their feelings. That, in turn, leads to questions that help students think about next steps—what actions they can take in response to a situation, who they can turn to when they need to talk, what things would help them feel better. These conversations guide students to resilience skills that will serve them throughout their lives.

Second, the two-rules questions guide students to deeper levels of empathy when the questions become "How can I help someone else feel good? How can I help someone else feel safe?" That level of exploration was useful for staff as they talked with students in the weeks after the tragedy. Together, students and staff came up with many ideas about how they could do things to support Dillon so he would feel safe and comfortable at school. Our students learned some basic skills the kinds of things people can do to help someone who is grieving after the loss of a loved one.

Third, it is important for educators and teachers to remember that they cannot know how much a student is depending on them after a trauma. Something as basic as the fact that the homeroom teacher follows the same exact routine every morning may provide a structure that a student is clinging to while they process overwhelming feelings. I didn't know that Dillon was carrying a huge burden of guilt after his brother's death. I was focusing on being a steady presence for him while he regrouped. But I was the only adult he felt safe enough with to allow his deepest hurt to surface. He knew he could trust me because I had presented to him as a steady, predictable, caring adult every day for over a year.

Supporting Staff through Trauma

Some teachers try hard to help students and burn out quickly from the added emotional work and a lack of knowledge about what works best for specific needs. Sociologist Susan E. Craig, who has studied the effects of childhood trauma for decades, points out that this can cause trauma and burnout for teachers. In her book *Trauma-Sensitive Schools: Learning Communities Transforming Children's Lives, K–5,* she wrote, "In the absence of trauma-specific training, teachers fail to recognize trauma's symptoms and lack the resources to reverse its course. When teachers come to believe that there is nothing they can do to effect changes in children's behaviors, they give up trying."[3]

Twenty years ago, there was almost no information about how to work with traumatized students. Today there is a rich and growing science-based literature about teaching approaches that support young brains affected by trauma. We know how to do it. But teachers need support and training in trauma-informed pedagogies. It is exhausting and debilitating to try to learn techniques on the job without the support of training.

Currently, at the end of 2022, twenty-seven states and the District of Columbia require trauma training for teachers. However, legislators have interpreted trauma training in widely diverse ways. For example, one state requires only one hour of training in "trauma-informed approaches." The law doesn't specify approaches to *what*. Another state doesn't provide trauma training every year; its law requires that 25 percent of teacher training every five years covers trauma-informed education for students dealing with grief and trauma. Conceivably, a teacher who worked in a district for fewer than five years or who moved across districts in that state every few years could miss out completely in training in that area. Another state requires teachers to "complete a mental health awareness training or similar program at least once." That statement is so vague and general that teachers may or may not receive training they urgently need. In the United States, there is a piecemeal approach to trauma training for teachers. Almost half the states have no requirement at all, and states that do sometimes have laws that aren't specific or comprehensive enough to truly meet the needs of trauma-affected children.[4]

As a result, it falls to principals to be proactive about gathering and providing resources to help teachers learn about ways of addressing trauma in their pedagogy. One way to do this is to accumulate your own library of books, pamphlets, and videos on trauma-informed pedagogy that teachers can borrow from. When a teacher encounters a specific situation in their classroom, they can use the library to learn about pedagogical approaches that would support students with ACEs. Another approach is to have staff all read one particular book or other resource and then discuss it in a staff meeting where teachers can learn from each other which strategies have worked for them (and which ones haven't). A third approach is to invite a professional from the community with expertise in trauma-informed pedagogy to give a workshop on a teacher development day. A nearby college or university with an education department or psychology department is a good place to look for an expert.

Every principal should canvas their community to identify resources that are available to struggling children and their families. Know which agencies provide counseling for free or on a sliding scale. Know where families can go when they need clothing. Know which churches and organizations provide food for families in need. Know where parents can access low-cost transportation to appointments and interviews. Know where parents can go to find information about employment. Know which local college or university offers courses that can help a parent upskill and learn if there are grants parents are eligible for. Know where the organizations are for your students' age group and talk with the leaders of those groups. Call every organization and institution that might have resources, even if information doesn't pop up on a website. Explore every nook and cranny of your community. Compile a list of names of organizations, phone numbers, and URLs and distribute it to your faculty. They will need that list so they can give information to parents during parent-teacher conferences. Keep this list top of mind for your staff by mentioning specific resources in your faculty newsletter. Mention these resources in newsletters for parents, on your school website, and in family meetings as appropriate.

I did one thing for nine years that was very successful. I invited professionals to the school for a student and staff workshop day related to mental health. (You can see how we organized a similar workshop in Appendix B.) One person came to talk about the dangers of depression. Another person came from the local rape crisis center. I had someone come from the YMCA to talk about the connection between exercise and well-being. I generally had at least six professionals for these workshops. I brought in people who were qualified to talk about the issues that were timely and relevant for our school.

Each expert participant was based in their own location in the school—one was in the gym, one was in the cafeteria, and so forth. We would begin the day with a keynote speaker who would introduce students and staff to the topics they would be learning about. Then students and staff *together* would move through the rooms according to a schedule our Building Leadership Team had prepared. It was important for teachers and students to hear the presentations together. Teachers heard the questions students asked and students heard the questions teachers asked. These workshop days gave teachers insights into what students were experiencing and thinking and students saw how much teachers cared about helping them.

How Trauma Shows Up in Classrooms

The number of households in the United States that can be classified as middle class has changed dramatically since the 1960s. From the late 1960s to 1980, over 30 percent of households living in poverty moved into the middle class.[5] By 1971, 61 percent of American households were classified in the middle income group. Four decades later, in 2021, the middle income group had decreased to 50 percent of households and the percentage in the lower income group had increased.[6] The

Covid-19 pandemic has had a sharp impact on the number of children living in poverty. From December 2021 to February 2022, the number of children in the country living in poverty increased by an astonishing 3.4 million.[7]

These numbers mean two things that principals should pay attention to. First, the long trajectory of a shrinking middle class means that some of the teachers in your building likely had poverty-related adverse experiences in childhood. Some of your staff may be carrying wounds from childhood that may surface unexpectedly in some situations they encounter with students. The long time frame of the shrinking middle class also means that the parents of many children carry wounds from their own ACEs. Second, children in classrooms across the nation are struggling to cope with high levels of anxiety about daily life needs, such as clean clothes, a safe place to sleep, access to meals, and a quiet place to regroup. And poverty is not the only predictor of ACEs for children. Violence, sexual abuse, and emotional abuse can be present in any household regardless of economic status.

Add to this the stress and anxiety the worldwide pandemic has caused. I'm sure each person reading this book has first-hand knowledge of what that has meant in classrooms. I'm sure you are all very familiar with this list of how ACEs show up in the behavior of kids at school (Figure 5.1).

Let's take a look at how just one type of adverse experience affects learning. Children who have witnessed violence may have neurological changes that alter how their brains function. They may have trouble storing information in short-term memory. Their executive function—their ability to organize and synthesize information—may be weakened. The way they process language may be compromised. Their reading ability may be lowered. They may have difficulty regulating their emotions. These brain changes harm their ability to focus and learn while they are in school. The behaviors students who have witnessed violence may exhibit are likely to result in labels that will haunt them for the rest

Figure 5.1. *Signs that students experiencing adverse circumstances need help*

Problems with communication and language; depressed vocabulary

Problems regulating emotions

Problems organizing their thoughts or belongings

Problems with hyper-arousal or low arousal

Problems sustaining attention or effort

Problems with acting before thinking

Problems with working memory

Inability to control inhibitions/distractions

Lack of empathy for others

Problems with forming bonds

Resistance to engagement with adults or attaching too quickly

Source: Betsy Rosenbalm, "Supporting Students with Adverse Childhood Experiences," EdNC, October 4, 2018, https://www.ednc.org/supporting-students-with-adverse-childhood-experiences.

of their years in the education system: ADHD, oppositional defiance disorder, or conduct disorder. They are twice as likely as other students to be referred to special education.[8]

Professional development for staff about ways they can interact with students who are experiencing or have experienced trauma will give teachers confidence about their classroom skills. But providing training about trauma-informed pedagogy is not the only way you can support staff. Helping staff become aware of how their own adverse childhood experiences may have created triggers that can be obstacles in their interactions with students is another important element of professional development. You may feel that this is beyond your ability. If that is the case, bring in a psychologist with expertise in helping adults heal from childhood trauma to provide information and suggestions about how to cope with triggers.

Caring for Yourself during Trauma

One of the best things you can do for yourself is prepare for trauma. Learn the death rituals of the communities and religious groups represented in your school. Learn as much as you can about the families of your students and try to have at least one face-to-face contact with them so you won't be a stranger walking into their home when a student dies. Know what your district can do to support you when there is a death in your school. Meet the members of the district's crisis intervention team.

Have a toolkit ready that consists of template letters to send to parents and to the media. When a crisis or trauma happens, you will be dealing with big emotions and it will be difficult to focus on tasks like writing a letter. You don't want to make a misstep in anything you say in a letter because you're struggling to manage your own emotional load. You should have letters for the death of a student, the death of a teacher or staff member, a natural disaster, or a public health issue. All you will need to do is enter specific details to get the letters ready to send (see Figure 5.2). The letter to students should be framed in language they can understand and should focus on their feelings. This letter from you should be read aloud to students. Either the homeroom teacher can read it first thing in the morning or the whole school can hear it at the same time during an all-school assembly. You will know what is best for your students. Have people in place for students to talk with immediately after this letter is read to them (see Figure 5.3).

Know what steps you will take in response to a crisis or trauma and in what order you should do them. Have a document on your computer

Figure 5.2. *Sample template letter to families after the death of a student, teacher, or staff member*

[DATE]

Dear Families,

It is with deep regret that we inform you about a recent loss to our school community. On [DATE], [NAME OF DECEASED] [INSERT BRIEF FACTS ABOUT THE DEATH]. This loss is sure to raise many emotions, concerns, and questions for our entire school, especially our students.

Our district has a Crisis Intervention Team made up of professionals trained to help with the needs of students, parents, and school personnel at difficult times such as this. This team will be leading us as we work together to address all of our needs. At our school, we will have additional counselors available for any student who may need or want help or any type of assistance surrounding this loss. We encourage you, as parents, to also feel free to use our resources.

We have enclosed some information that may be useful to you in helping your child/children at home. If you would like additional information or need assistance, please do not hesitate to contact our district Crisis Intervention Team Leader at [PHONE NUMBER AND/OR EMAIL].

We are saddened by the loss to our school community and will make every effort to help you and your child/children as you need.

Sincerely,

PRINCIPAL [TYPE AND SIGN YOUR NAME]

Figure 5.3 *Sample template letter to students after the death of a student, teacher, or staff member*

Dear Students:

I have asked that we all receive this information at the same time together this morning. It sadness me to let you know that [NAME OF DECEASED] has died. [SENTENCE THAT SAYS WHEN IT HAPPENED AND INCLUDES DETAILS THAT CAN BE SHARED WITH STUDENTS.]

This news can be difficult for us to understand. Hearing about the death of someone close to us brings many emotions for us to try to understand. We are all here to help and support you with the feelings you may be experiencing. Our school will have many extra resources available to support all of us.

The District Crisis Response Team is [PLACE WHERE THEY ARE LOCATED] to meet with you if you are in need to talk with someone. The team will be available all day to support you. I want to encourage you to seek out these members if you are struggling in any way. It is okay to have these feelings of grief and we care about all of you.

and in hard copy (in case there is a power outage) that outlines these steps.

Review the school leader entry plan from your state principals' association. Make sure you have completed all of the steps to prepare for trauma.

You will need support during a trauma. Develop a network of administrator colleagues that you can turn to. One twenty-minute phone call with someone who has experience with something you're going through can make all the difference in your ability to cope emotionally during a crisis.

Recognize that when you're leading a school through trauma, you are not in normal life. You may not be able to keep your usual routine because you will need to prioritize basic physical needs like good nutrition, enough sleep, or getting exercise.

Resource List

Susan Craig, *Trauma-Sensitive Schools for the Adolescent Years: Promoting Resiliency and Healing, Grades 6–12* (Teachers College Press, 2017).

If you want to understand how trauma affects the teenage brain, this is the book for you. Chapters provide information about the effects of trauma on adolescent neural development, cognitive changes in response to trauma, and how trauma marginalizes students. Craig describes what schools and teachers can do to facilitate remodeling of the brain after trauma so that students can form secure attachments in adulthood. An especially valuable chapter looks at the effects of secondary trauma on teachers in the context of teacher attrition. The final chapter discusses steps a school can take as it moves toward a trauma-sensitive culture, including the things to be aware of during that shift. As the foreword notes, this book is "a sequential plan for implementation of a trauma-sensitive school."

Bill Ziegler, Dave Ramage, Andrea Parson, and Justin Foster, *Trauma-Sensitive School Leadership: Building a Learning Environment to Support Healing and Success* (ASCD, 2022).

This book is full of practical suggestions for leaders who are building a trauma-sensitive school. After a discussion of the biases and barriers to supporting learners who have experienced trauma, the book moves into topics that are relevant for a school principal's daily practices and plans. One chapter looks at how to plan all-school events and daily lesson plans in ways that will not retraumatize students. Other topics include avoiding discipline practices that perpetuate behaviors traumatized students may exhibit, designing physical spaces that foster a trauma-sensitive culture, and developing relationships with traumatized students that give them tools they need for self-care. There's an excellent chapter on learning to ask for help and another on secondary trauma as it relates to teachers.

Michael S. Gaskell, *Leading Schools through Trauma: A Data-Driven Approach to Helping Children Heal* (Routledge, 2022).

Michael Gaskell is a school principal who offers his colleagues information not covered in other books on leading through trauma. This book offers detailed suggestions about how to collect shorter-term data that will help educators identify student needs quickly. Gaskell also has a chapter on professional development for teachers about student trauma. His chapter on setting goals with students uses the lovely phrase "post-traumatic growth." One suggestion he offers for helping middle-school students contextualize their traumatic experiences is a program titled "I'm More Than Just That" in which high school students talk with middle school students about how they coped with and survived experiences with bullying, discrimination, racism, and other traumatic experiences when they were in middle school. This book is full of ideas for small, short actions and interventions to support students who have experienced trauma.

Suicide Prevention Resource Center, Education Development Center, and American Foundation for Suicide Prevention, *After a Suicide: A Toolkit for Schools*, 2nd ed. (2018), https://sprc.org/online-library/after-suicide-toolkit-schools.

The information in this free resource has been reviewed by psychiatrists, psychologists, physicians, epidemiologists, educators, and social workers. It offers extremely detailed information about how a school should respond when a student ends their life—who to talk to, who in the community has information you will need, what messages the school should send and to whom, what steps a school can take to help students cope, considerations for memorializing the student who has died, how to present information on social media, and identifying other students who are at risk for suicide. A valuable appendix has templates and tools that include guidelines for the first all-staff meeting, tips for talking about suicide, a sample agenda for meeting with parents, a sample media statement, key messages for the media spokesperson, facts about suicide in adolescents, warning signs, and what to do in a crisis.

6

Using Teams to Support the Whole Child

The teams gave us additional support for students who needed more than we could offer in the time we had to address them. The intervention team took a lot off our plates and helped ensure that no students fell through the cracks.
—Fall Ridge Teacher

I knew that the mental health needs of Fall Ridge students were great. At a time when national estimates of students with mental health issues ranged from 10 to 30 percent, at least 75 percent of the students at our school exhibited signs of depression and anxiety.[1] I encountered the teen mental health crisis almost a decade before it became a national issue. These issues manifested in the kinds of behavioral issues educators are seeing on a large scale since students returned to classrooms after the Covid-19 pandemic. Classroom management was a big problem for many teachers, fights were common, hallway passing periods were noisy and boisterous, and students didn't seem interested in learning. For many students at Fall Ridge, being in school was just "doing time." Poverty was the underlying cause of much of what I saw in our school; our county had been hit hard by major economic change for over a decade.

In the first decade of this century, researchers didn't often speak about the mental *health* of teens. When the mental health of students was addressed in the literature, it was framed as "psychiatric disorders," the kinds of mental illness that require medical treatment. Or it was framed as the behavioral outcomes of mental health that has been disrupted by trauma and adversity. The questions researchers asked were "How can we prevent delinquency? How can we prevent smoking and drug use? How can we prevent dropouts?" In my mind, these were twentieth-century questions that were out of date. They didn't ask the only question that interested me: "How can we create a school environment that supports the mental health of our students?" I wanted a school environment that nurtured students and prevented problems.

The situation in our school had overwhelmed several of my predecessors. Most had lasted at Fall Ridge for only a couple of years. But I approached the problem with the question I have always used when faced with a challenge in my job. Instead of saying, "This situation is impossible. There's no way I can meet the needs of these kids with the resources I have," I asked, "How can we meet the emotional and mental health needs of these students with the resources we have?" My answer was that we would use our teams as part of a network that monitored the well-being of each student every day.

Creating a school environment that provided the components of mental health—feeling good and feeling safe at school—wasn't high on the agenda of many educators. In 2000, two researchers at the UCLA Center for Mental Health in Schools noted that "the continuing trend is for schools and districts to treat [pupil services and school health programs], in policy and practice, as desirable but not essential." Staff and programs that supported student mental health were marginalized, planning for such services was "done on an ad hoc basis," and "specialist personnel almost never [were] a prominent part of a school's organizational structure."[2]

I wanted an organizational structure in our school that flipped the current practices in most schools at the time. I was determined to make student mental health the center of our mission and to make the staff and specialized professionals who could support that goal integral to every aspect of the education we delivered.

A Team Structure to Serve the Whole Child

When I was hired as principal at Fall Ridge, I negotiated with the district to introduce a team structure in our building. Instead of a junior high school, we would be a middle school. I was convinced that this approach would support students in the school culture I wanted to create. I came to the middle school with the chart you see in Figure 6.1 on the following page. I served my first year at a junior high school without utilizing a team approach. After observing what school culture was like for students in that school, I knew what kind of structure I wanted and I was quite sure it would work. I came to Fall Ridge with the organizational chart I wanted already clear in my mind.

In our approach, teams focused on the emotional needs of our students as much as they did on academics. We devoted intensive attention to academics. We taught our students the practical and executive skills they needed to learn. Our teachers worked hard to improve their classroom skills and to learn new skills that responded to the academic needs they saw. We had multiple programs in place to support academic learning and we made changes and introduced new programs in response to what we observed. Teachers requested specific types of professional development and I worked hard to see that they got it. But we did all of that through a lens of awareness of the emotional and social needs of our students. This was based on the strong beliefs that if a student was struggling emotionally, they would also struggle academically and that meeting the emotional needs of students would remove a barrier to learning.

One teacher recalls that the team approach we used at Fall Ridge was focused on creating a feeling of family with the students Grade-Level Teams monitored. She has also worked in teams organized by teaching area that focus on academics. She feels that what she calls the "families team structure" is more effective: "We worked within our team to make connections with kids, know their strengths and weaknesses, and come up with both behavioral and academic strategies to help them. As we made these kids part of our 'family,' we saw students

Figure 6.1. *Organization of teams in a two-rules school*

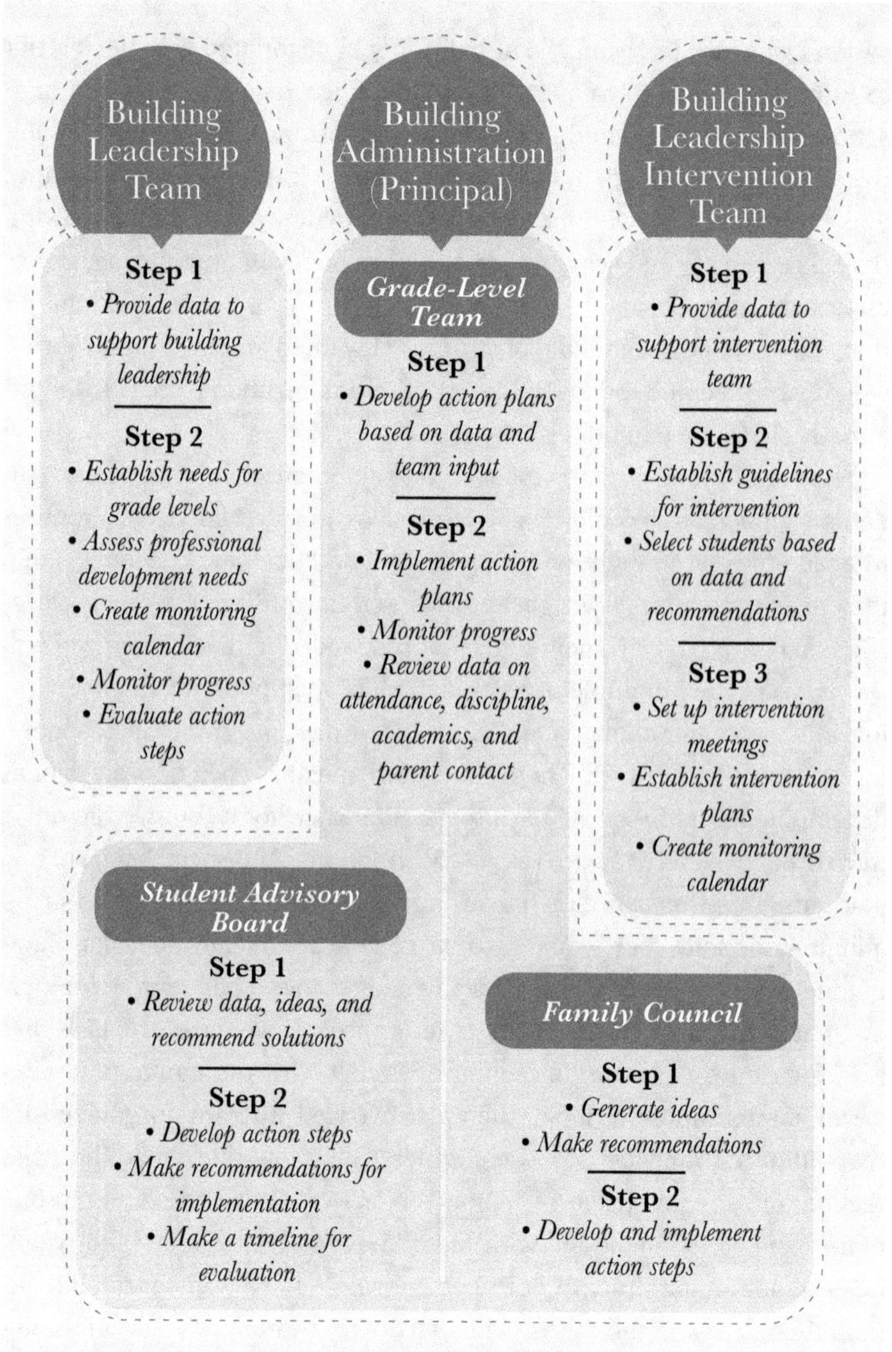

Building Leadership Team

Step 1
- *Provide data to support building leadership*

Step 2
- *Establish needs for grade levels*
- *Assess professional development needs*
- *Create monitoring calendar*
- *Monitor progress*
- *Evaluate action steps*

Building Administration (Principal)

Grade-Level Team

Step 1
- *Develop action plans based on data and team input*

Step 2
- *Implement action plans*
- *Monitor progress*
- *Review data on attendance, discipline, academics, and parent contact*

Building Leadership Intervention Team

Step 1
- *Provide data to support intervention team*

Step 2
- *Establish guidelines for intervention*
- *Select students based on data and recommendations*

Step 3
- *Set up intervention meetings*
- *Establish intervention plans*
- *Create monitoring calendar*

Student Advisory Board

Step 1
- *Review data, ideas, and recommend solutions*

Step 2
- *Develop action steps*
- *Make recommendations for implementation*
- *Make a timeline for evaluation*

Family Council

Step 1
- *Generate ideas*
- *Make recommendations*

Step 2
- *Develop and implement action steps*

become more invested in their success." This teacher also notes that "teachers felt supported by other staff members" on their team. "Both staff and students seemed much happier," she recalls. "The whole building was like a big family."[3]

Grade-Level Teams

The foundation of our team structure was the Grade-Level Teams of two, three, or four teachers. Each team member was the homeroom teacher for 20 to 25 students. For grades seven and eight, teams of three and four taught the homeroom students of all of the team members. So each team was monitoring the academic performance and mental health of 75 to 100 students over the course of the day. Students came together in homeroom at the beginning of the day and traveled together during the day to classes in core academic areas, which the teachers on their team taught. Because of this structure, three or four teachers had a close eye on the academic, emotional, and social state of every student at Fall Ridge every day. These teacher teams were staff with "boots on the ground" who often were able to pick up on signs that a student was in distress at an early stage.

Our monitoring of students' well-being began the moment they got off the bus. I was always there to greet each student by name. I was equipped with a radio that communicated with the school resource officer. My assistant principal, the dean of students, my secretary, the school social worker, and the head custodian also had radios. Two teachers, team leaders who rotated in this duty, also had radios. One was in the front of the school and the other was in the back. This network watched as students entered the building. When they observed a student exhibiting signs of anxiety or depression, one of these people would alert that student's Grade-Level Team leader by radio so the team would know before homeroom period started that they should work to help that student have a good day. If the student was in acute distress, the message went directly to the school social worker or the school psychologist. All of these adults had eyes on our students so they could catch signs of distress as soon as possible.

During the day, the Grade-Level Team members monitored for signs of distress as they taught their classes. They were trained to notice signs of anxiety and depression as they manifest at school (see Figure 6.2) and to gauge how acute a student's distress was. (I have included the signs of depression in both children and adolescents because it is often the case that a depressed teen will regress in some behaviors.) Signs of depression can be detected in every aspect of a student's demeanor and behavior and staff should be trained to recognize them. As a school psychologist and a professor of education have noted, "Depressed students often give up more quickly on tasks they perceive as daunting, refuse to attempt academic work they find too difficult, and quickly doubt their ability to independently complete academic tasks or solve problems. Memory, speech, physical and motor activity, and the ability to plan may also be affected. Many depressed children and adolescents are lethargic, speak laboriously, and have difficulty completely expressing thoughts and ideas."[4]

Figure 6.2. *Characteristics of depression in children and adolescents*

CHARACTERISTICS	WHAT IT LOOKS LIKE IN SCHOOL
Physical/somatic complaints	Complaints of feeling sick, school absence, lack of participation, sleepiness
Irritability	Isolation from peers, problems with social skills, defiance
Difficulty concentrating on tasks/activities	Poor work completion
Short-term memory impairment	Forgetting to complete assignments, difficulty concentrating
Difficulties with planning, organizing, and executing tasks	Refusing to complete work, missing deadlines
Facial expressions or body language indicating depression or sadness	Working slowly

(continues)

Figure 6.2. *Continued*

CHARACTERISTICS	WHAT IT LOOKS LIKE IN SCHOOL
Hypersensitivity	Easily hurt feelings, crying, anger
Poor performance and follow-through on tasks	Poor work completion
Inattention	Distractibility, restlessness
Forgetfulness	Poor work submission, variable academic performance
Separation anxiety from parents or caregivers	Crying, somatic complaints, frequent absences, school refusal
Decreased self-esteem or feelings of self-worth	Self-deprecating comments
Mild irritability	Defiance with authority figures, difficulties interacting with peers, argumentative
Negative perceptions of student's past and present	Pessimistic comments, suicidal thoughts
Peer rejection	Isolation, frequent change in friends
Lack of interest and involvement in previously enjoyed activities	Isolation and withdrawal
Boredom	Sulking, noncompliance
Impulsive and risky behavior	Theft, sexual activity, alcohol or drug use, truancy
Substance abuse	Acting out of character, sleeping in class

Source: R. Marc A. Crundwell and Kim Killu, "Responding to a Student's Depression," *ACSD* 68, no. 2 (2010), https://www.ascd.org/el/articles/responding-to-a-students-depression.

We integrated attention to mental health with academics seamlessly. For example, a language arts teacher and a social studies teacher on the same Grade-Level Team might notice that a student was struggling with reading comprehension. Those team members would begin a series of interventions. The first would be making sure a reading assignment matched the reading level of the student. If the student couldn't answer questions that demonstrated comprehension after that intervention, the team would add reading the text aloud to the student. If the student was still struggling, the student's team would set up a meeting for the student with the school social worker to learn if a situation at home was creating high stress levels. If that wasn't the case, the team would contact the school psychologist to discuss testing to identify a learning or processing difference. If testing revealed a learning difficulty, the Building Leadership Intervention Team would be notified and the school would work with the family to connect them to external services.

Grade-Level Teams met every day to compare notes on what team members had observed, discuss their curricular plans for the next day, and plan interventions to support students having difficulty of any kind—academic, behavioral, or emotional. They also supported each other; if one member was having difficulty completing a task the team was responsible for, their colleagues would step up to help them. As one teacher on a Grade-Level Team recalls, "We would work together to get missing work done or contact parents. We would divide and conquer all our tasks for our kids." At the end of every day, Grade-Level Teams fed crucial data to me, to the Building Leadership Team, and to the Building Leadership Intervention Team. Data was conveyed in real time on a shared server.

At Fall Ridge, a student in acute distress was immediately connected with either the social worker or the school psychologist and sometimes with both (see Figure 6.3). Teams would try several strategies to help students whose behavior indicated lower levels of distress, monitoring the results of those strategies for several days. If none of the Grade-Level Team's strategies worked, they would alert the Building Leadership Intervention Team, a group of professionals with specialized skills who could connect a student and their family with community organizations that could support them. (The Building Leadership Intervention Team is discussed later in this chapter.)

Figure 6.3. *Examples of mental health interventions of Grade-Level Teams*

STUDENT BEHAVIOR	INTERVENTION EXAMPLE
Not completing homework	Ask the student to attend a team meeting to learn if the team can do something to help with getting assignments completed.
Student falling asleep in class throughout the day	Refer to school nurse and school social worker to identify the reason. Based on their answers, student may be referred to Building Leadership Intervention Team to connect the student and their family with community professionals who can help.
Sudden onset of difficulty with executive function (e.g., organizing notes and assignments)	This is an indication that the student may be experiencing anxiety, depression, PTSD, or a new trauma. A visit with the social worker or the school psychologist would be the first step.
Onset of irritability, withdrawal	These are red flags for depression and the potential of self-harm or harm to others. Immediate referral to school social worker and school psychologist.
Fight with best friend	Social-emotional welfare is a critical aspect of a middle school student's life and a disruption in a social network is a serious event. Grade-Level Team checks to see which adults in the building have an established relationship with the student so they can meet with them to listen.

Responding to Crisis

We know that a school that intervenes early with a student experiencing depression and anxiety can reduce their mental health burden. A 2017 meta-analysis of the effects of school-based treatment for teens with depression and anxiety showed that teachers and trained mental health professionals at school can help students experiencing anxiety and that support at school in combination with referral to mental health professionals in the community is the best strategy for students experiencing depression.[5] The stakes are high: in 2022, suicide was the second-largest cause of death for young people aged 10–24 in the United States.[6] Even students that seem to be thriving can be crushed by one adverse event. As I was writing this book, the nation learned the heartbreaking story of a teenage girl who was happy, was close with her large family, and was close with her neighbors' young children (she had even rescued one of them from drowning one time). But one day at school, a gang of girls attacked her and the attack was video-recorded. The girl knew the video would be seen by everyone in her school. She told her father that she didn't want to be seen as the girl who got beat up at school, and in the middle of the night after the attack, she died by suicide.[7] This tragedy illustrates the urgent need for schools to respond immediately and decisively to bullying incidents. The young woman in this event was so devastated by what she perceived as the loss of the image she wanted to project at school that she felt she could not survive the embarrassmen and took action within less than 24 hours.

We all know that in a moment of crisis, the mind can go blank. In situations where rapid response is required, it's important to have information about what to do close at hand. At Fall Ridge, every classroom had a paper document with the numbers to call for the types of crisis situations teachers were likely to encounter. In addition, we had policies in place for how the school would respond to crises that touched students' lives. Several times when I was writing this book, I learned of bullying situations that caused serious physical and emotional harm to students. When the parents of the bullied student contacted the school for support, the response was that the school couldn't help them. That is never an acceptable response to a crisis. Have a plan in place for how your school will respond with compassion and support for mental health when a crisis occurs. Figure 6.4 shows examples of plans we had in place at Fall Ridge.

Figure 6.4. *Fall Ridge plans for principal responses to emergency situations*

Situation
A student has a meltdown during the school day (uncontrolled rage, crying, complete shutdown)

Response Plan
When a child demonstrates this type of behavior, we looked first to see if this had happened before. Then we asked the school social worker and school psychologist to work with the student. If those staff members weren't on campus, I would work with the student to see if they would talk. I would always wait much longer to hear the student's responses than is typical. Middle school students are still learning how to collect and present their thoughts and when they are upset, that task is much more difficult for them.

Based on the information I gathered, I would call the family to let them know about what happened. I would provide information about resources in the community if they want to seek out additional support.

Situation
Staff is notified that a family is in a crisis situation

Response Plan
Example: The Grade-Level Team leader reports they have learned that their student is now homeless. They know they have younger siblings in another school. They are worried about the family.

(continued)

Figure 6.4. *Continued*

Principal asks the social worker to talk with the student and to contact the social worker(s) at the sibling(s) school(s). If you do not have a school social worker, the principal or assistant principal will reach out to the community groups that help families in need. They will work together to help the family find temporary shelter, food, and clothing.

School works to help students with their needs at school by supporting them with a trusted adult who checks on them daily as they arrive at school and at the end of the day.

Situation
A death in the student's family

Response Plan
Principal asks the social worker and school psychologist to come to the office to speak about the situation. Principal calls an all-staff meeting to talk to inform staff, to let them know that other students in the building may be related to the family, and to ask them to contact the school social worker if they hear or see children having difficulties or talking about this situation. Principal asks staff to collect names of students who may want to participate in a grief group.

Situation
A student threatens suicide

Response Plan
Take any form of suicide threat seriously. If a student says to a friend, a teacher, or an administrator that they want to kill themselves, they must come to the office immediately.

Principal will call the local agency that works with suicide prevention. Principal calls a family member to the school and advises them of the situation when they arrive. At that meeting, principal provides options for counseling services and makes a plan with the family member for support at school.

(continued)

Figure 6.4. *Continued*

Situation

A student attempts suicide

Response Plan

Principal speaks with family and the students. Works with school psychologist or contract psychologist to collect information on strategies, resources, or tools the school can use to support the student. Plan will be established with the student's Grade-Level Team and the elective teachers the student sees daily. A trusted adult of the student's choice will check in with the student at the beginning and end of each day. A follow-up meeting is scheduled for one week later.

Situation

A student ends their life

Response Plan

When a student ends their life, it sets off a ripple of waves that flows through the entire community. It moves very rapidly and can become ocean waves quickly. Always have a template ready for a letter of condolence to the family from you and from the school. In moments of high emotion, it is difficult to collect the thoughts you want to convey in such a letter. Have that template ready so all you have to do is add specific details about the student.

Call the teachers of the student who has died and ask if you can stop by to see them. Tell them in person what has happened. Remind them of the plan the school has in place for responding to this situation. Speak with compassion and remind the teachers of the support that is available to them through the school.

Contact the district to request additional social workers. Ask for help from outside agencies also. Make sure you will have enough support for students and staff in the next week or so.

(continued)

Figure 6.4. *Continued*

Ask the district for floating substitute teachers so they can relieve staff who want to speak with counselors.

Call an all-school assembly to address the students together and introduce all of the support staff who have joined their school family on that day to help them.

Situation

A student makes threatening statements about doing harm to others or wanting to do harm to others

Response Plan

Always take a threat seriously. Instruct teachers to contact the office immediately when they hear a threat and have the student escorted to the office. Have the student's locker searched. Ask the student to empty their pockets. Ask the student about the threats they have made.

Contact a family member immediately and ask them to come to the school.

If the student has brought a gun to school, contact the police department so an officer can be present at the meeting with the family member. The next steps you take will be guided by the decision the police officer makes about the situation.

Document this meeting.

Follow up with the student and their family.

Situation

A physical attack takes place in the lunch area. Three students attack one girl.

Response Plan

Students are referred to the principal's office. Medical care is provided to students in need.

(continued)

Figure 6.4. *Continued*

Because this is a mob action against a student, principal contacts police and family members of students.

Gather the facts: give students, including bystanders, opportunities to write statements about what they did or saw. Social worker can follow up with sessions. Advise parents of counselor support available.

Determine if any other students are connected to the incident. Ask the school resource officer to talk with students to gain additional information about the incident and to talk with students about the incident.

Situation

Five students become ill and one says they all took something another student gave them

Response Plan

Call for medical support.

Contact families of ill students.

Locate what the students took to provide to the medical staff treating students.

Call in drug counselors to talk with all students about not taking something when you do not know what it is.

Send a letter home with students. Follow up with email or robocall in case the letter doesn't get to parents. Convey to parents that students at your school are safe and remind them to have conversations with their children about safety. Place a message on school website about when and where drug counseling will be available if families are interested in knowing more or would like to speak to a drug counselor.

The Building Leadership Team

Membership on the Building Leadership Team was a paid position because this team met after the contractual school day. Teachers applied for these positions and the members were carefully selected for their skills. The team consisted of two Grade-Level Team leaders from each grade level, one special education professional, and one teacher of one of the electives (e.g., computer science, music, other languages). It was important to weed out applicants for this team who only wanted to do it for the money. I would ask candidates "What are you going to contribute? What are your goals? Where do you think the school needs to go?" I would find out what strengths the candidates had. For example, some people were able to help with the Positive Behavior and Intervention Supports (PBIS) program. Some were good at scheduling. Some were good at public relations; they would encourage Grade-Level Team leaders to share information and artifacts about what was happening in the building so they could promote that information with local media. Some had strong connections with community members and institutions that could help with fundraising.

The Building Leadership Team was responsible for having its finger on the pulse of the building. They collected building-wide discipline data from the dean of students. They collected data on test results and grades from the school guidance counselor. They collected attendance data from the attendance office. They used this data to identify "hot spots" in the operation of the school. For example, they could identify if truancy was higher on particular days. They could identify if a teacher's approach was generating a higher number of discipline issues with students. This team also had access to the school social worker and the county truancy officer; these two professionals attended meetings of the Building Leadership Team as needed.

Another professional who was helpful to the Building Leadership Team was our school resource officer. The dean of students envisioned the school resource officer as a "hammer"; as someone who cracked down on bad behavior and enforced the rules. That's not how I saw the role of the school resource officer at all. I wanted our resource officer to be a trusted adult our students could talk to, someone whose door was always open to kids who needed help. I made sure our resource officer had an office that students could go to when they wanted to talk with him.

It took some time to convince the Building Leadership Team and our school resource officer that my vision for the resource officer could work to benefit everyone in the building. I met with both the Building Leadership Team and the resource officer to explain that I wanted the presence of a resource officer in our building to be a positive experience for everyone. I told him about the two-rules process for dealing with problems among the students. It took him some time to shift his thinking about his role. He initially thought of the students as potential lawbreakers who needed strong discipline, but after watching the close relationships students had with me and with their teachers, he began to see them as human beings who needed nurturing and support.

After that mental shift, he worked hard to build good rapport with the students. His office became a resource for students who needed a cool-down spot or someone to talk to. To facilitate stronger relationships with the students, I asked him to be present at every school lunch hour. At first he thought I was diminishing his role, but I assured him that the lunch room was the best place to get to know each student. I told him that he would often see me in the cafeteria, sitting down and talking with kids or viewing their video presentations on the pull-down screen.

Because of his reconfigured role, our school resource officer became a valuable source of information for the Building Leadership Team. His approach was very much one of community policing—building relationships so police can work with community members to proactively solve problems. He developed warm relationships with every student and gave particular attention to students in special education. "Nobody else was going to give those kids extra attention, so I made them my priority," he recalls. He had an office in our building where he always kept a jar of lollipops. Kids stopped in to talk with him in that private space every day. He would often hear from them about planned shootings in the neighborhoods and would pass the information along to his colleagues so they could prevent them.

OT, as he was known to students (a nickname based on "O" for "Officer" and the first initial of his last name), was a great asset for our mental health monitoring approach. He would approach a struggling kid about to have a meltdown, put his arm around their shoulders, and say "Let's take a walk." They would walk and talk until the student had calmed down. Our students loved him and thought of him as their true friend. He learned valuable information about students' mental states from his daily interactions and often passed details about that topic to the Building Leadership Team that team members might not have learned any other way. His community policing approach and his deep caring went a long way toward making our students feel good and feel safe every day.

Based on the data the Building Leadership Team collected, team members created action plans for dealing with issues related to attendance, academics, and discipline. They also collected data from the Grade-Level Teams about the types of professional development teachers were requesting. Sometimes the Building Leadership Team identified a particular skill that would help teachers respond to an issue they were encountering. When that happened, they would request a training workshop or access to external resources that would give teachers the skill they needed.

The Building Leadership Team kept on top of many issues that traditionally were seen as the principal's role. Because of their work, I was able to craft my role as principal in a way that focused on building and strengthening the relationships of trust that were so crucial to the success of our two-rules school. I had time to teach students experiencing difficulty what it meant to feel good and feel safe. This was especially important for students who had violated our two rules. Whenever possible, instead of sending students directly to the dean of students for discipline, I would spend time mentoring students about friendship, empathy, trust, and community. I was able to do this because of the hard work the Building Leadership Team members did for our school.

Building Leadership Intervention Team

Our Building Leadership Intervention Team functioned as a safety net for students who were experiencing trauma or inadequate care at home. Our philosophy was that early intervention could prevent harm and help a student negotiate difficult circumstances that threatened to upend their progress as students and as young people trying to develop toward a successful adulthood.

The team consisted of seven people: my assistant principal, the school guidance counselor, the school psychologist, the school social worker, the school resource officer, the county truancy officer, and a teacher who rotated in depending on the grade level we were discussing.

This team could move swiftly when the school became aware of trauma in a student's life. For example, say that a teacher overhears a custodian telling a seventh grade student that he has learned during his lunch hour that her mother had a psychotic break that morning and tried to drown herself and her two youngest children. The custodian knows this because he is friends with this student's next-door neighbors and has lunch at their house every day. So the student has learned of deep trauma even before she hears of it from a family member. The teacher would immediately report this information to me or to my assistant principal, who would immediately inform the Building Leadership Intervention Team. Since this is a secondhand report, the first step would be to learn what happened and confirm the details. We would want to know if the police were involved. We would need to know if any other agencies are involved with this incident. If the police were involved, we would want to know if they could share any information about the incident with us that would help us plan our support strategy. We would ask questions such as "Are the two young children safe? Is someone caring for them? Did the mother get the medical attention she needs? Is she hospitalized? Does the father have the resources to care for the other children in the family?

Do other children in the family besides the seventh-grade student know what happened?" After collecting information, the intervention team would schedule an immediate meeting to strategize about who else to involve in support for this family.

The team's first concern would be to establish immediate supports for the student, who would be struggling to process issues beyond her understanding. The team would ask the Grade-Level Team to handle this issue very sensitively. In conversations with the father, the Building Leadership Intervention Team has learned that he doesn't want the public to know that his wife tried to drown herself and two babies. The story he is telling is that his wife had a nervous breakdown. The school would want to respect this decision, so it would be important to convey this information to the Grade-Level Team of the student in our school. The Grade-Level Team's job is to monitor the seventh-grade student closely:

- How is her attendance?
- What are her current academics?
- Can the team provide information to the Building Leadership Team about her demeanor?
- Does she have friends?
- Has an adult at school built a relationship with her?

We would also ask the school social worker to introduce herself to the student and build a closer relationship with her. We would ask the school psychologist to do some shadowing to see how the student is doing in the school setting. We would see if the father was open to a family meeting with myself and the school social worker or the school psychologist to find out how the school could support the family. If the father was open to connections with community agencies, we could help the student and her family connect with organizations that could provide counseling to help them understand their new situation and process their feelings.

This is one example of how the Building Leadership Intervention Team would respond to acute trauma. "Intervention" was the key word in this team's name. This team of professionals worked to provide support at school and connections with community professionals who could help students and their families navigate their way through problems, challenges, and traumas.

Many of the cases our team worked on started out as truancy cases. As the team asked questions and gathered information, it often would become clear that a family was struggling with serious issues: homelessness, a single parent who was gravely ill, parents who needed mental health counseling, families that needed connections to social service and community agencies to help them cope with poverty. A home visit sometimes became a component of the Building Leadership Intervention Team's response. These were always done with myself and the school social worker or the county truancy officer. In these visits, we could show families that the school was there to help, not to judge.

The Importance of Community Connections

Connections with community agencies are an important element of providing mental health support for students. In your role as administrator, you will encounter students and families who need rapid help in an emergency. Ideally, you will have a school social worker who can facilitate links to community organizations. But you should also have this information at your fingertips; you never know when you will be the one who needs to make these connections.

The best way to form an alliance with community groups is to be involved with your community. Make a point of supporting community activities sponsored by potential allies. Learn how your school can contribute to fundraising for a community agency. Make a point of introducing yourself to leaders of local agencies and institutions and forming friendly professional relationships with them.

Don't make your first point of contact a phone call that asks for help for your school. That is a sure way to get shut down. As with everything else you do to create a positive school climate, it all starts with relationships.

Learn the network in your county for households facing sudden emergencies. Make sure you know what days and times local food pantries are open. Find out if there's a group that helps with transportation to and from pantries. Know who to call if a family experiences a fire. Know who to call if you learn that a student urgently needs clothing.

Below is a starter list of categories of community groups and institutions that are potential allies in your quest to provide the support your students need.

- Housing
- Women's shelters
- Men's shelters
- Department of Children and Family Services
- Clothing and food
- Local churches with food and clothing pantries
- Local United Way
- Mental health crises/mental health wellness
- Drug treatment and rehabilitation facilities
- Rape crisis centers
- Local suicide prevention hotlines
- Local health department
- Local organizations that focus on crisis recovery
- Family therapy
- Children's services centers/organizations
- Local chapter of National Alliance on Mental Illness
- Local department of social services
- Legal Help

- Local chapter of CASA (Court Appointed Legal Advocates)
- Peer (or youth) court
- Social/sports activities
- Big Brother/Big Sisters
- Boys and Girls Clubs
- YMCA

In addition, local groups organized on the basis of race, ethnicity, sexual identity, or nationality can help students develop a positive identity. Professors from local colleges and universities can show students possible futures.

Transparency and Teams

We were open with students about the multiple roles their Grade-Level Teams filled. Students were aware that the teachers on their team were interested in their well-being and were there to help. Most students were happy to have the extra attention.

When a student was in a situation that required the attention of the Building Leadership Intervention Team, we always let the student know that that team was working on their behalf. We would invite the student to attend the team meeting so the team members could hear about the situation from the student's perspective. If a parent or caregiver was willing to attend, we welcomed them too. We wanted students and their families who were in traumatic and emergency situations to know that a whole team of caring people was there to help and support them.

I was transparent and consistently clear about what I wanted each type of team to do. Several days before the Building Leadership Team meeting, I would send the agenda to team members. As our meeting time was limited to one class period, we knew that we needed to use that time wisely and efficiently. When the team knew the issues on the agenda, members could plan what they wanted to say in ways that would move the team closer to a decision about an action step. Similarly, when the Building Leadership Intervention Team needed to meet, members shared as much information as they knew before the meeting so we could focus on what a student was telling us (if the student was attending) and on our plan of action.

Accountability was also important to the success of our teams. Each time we planned an action step, we assigned a timeline to it. The Building Leadership Team and Grade-Level Teams might agree to check in after three weeks to see if an action step was working. If it wasn't, we would try a different strategy. We would keep repeating this process until we reached a strategy that worked. We never made plans that were just talk. All of our plans were clear commitments to take action on the part of students, teachers, and administration. We used this same strategy with the Building Leadership Intervention Team. After the student and their family member had agreed to a strategy the team suggested, we asked them to sign what we called an Assurance Contract that listed the steps that everyone had agreed to take. Those contracts always had a short timeline. We would meet again in two or three weeks to hear how things were going, what changes had been made, and what changes needed to be made to our agreement.

Teams for Students and Parents

So far I've been describing the teams that functioned within our building with administration, teachers, and other school professionals. Our Family Council and Student Advisory Board were groups that worked outside of our school. These were important ways of helping family members and students feel like they belonged to our school and that their ideas and opinions were heard.

Family Council

Our Family Council Team met once a month in the evening. Each meeting had a focused topic that family members received in advance, but we also had time at every meeting for family members and caregivers to voice ideas, thoughts, concerns, and celebrations. The Family Council discussed curriculum, discipline procedures and policies, attendance, safety, fundraising, field trips, and many other topics. We welcomed ideas and suggestions for discussion.

One member from our Family Council Team represented Fall Ridge at the district-level Family Council meetings. This was an opportunity for a parent or caregiver to present the Fall Ridge point of view at the district level and to bring back information about district-level plans.

One Grade-Level Team Leader was present at each Family Council meeting; teams rotated who would attend.

Student Advisory Board

Our Student Advisory Board worked with the assistant principal to share any ideas, concerns, or suggestions about ways to improve our school. Student members of this board looked at our school improvement plan and our mission and vision statement. They also saw grade-level data on academic performance, discipline, and attendance. Our food service director or building and grounds director oversaw this group of students.

This student board also met with the student advisory boards of other middle schools and the district's high school to look at the district as a whole. They generated ideas and suggestions about changes to recommend to the Board of Education. The student board chose which member would speak to the Board of Education with their final recommendations.

This was a place where students could learn about leadership and build capacity. Membership on this board helped students see the important role students had in the plans of the school and the district. Grade-Level Teams recommended students for board membership, making sure that students of all backgrounds had an opportunity to serve. The Building Leadership Team interviewed the students the Grade-Level Teams recommended.

The Importance of School Psychologists

The school psychologist played a pivotal role in the team structure at Fall Ridge. We were very fortunate to have this position filled on a full-time basis. In 2023, we all know that it is difficult to hire a school psychologist because of a severe staffing shortage. Nevertheless, a full-time school psychologist is the ideal. I want to take a moment to point out

Figure 6.5 *School psychologist competencies*

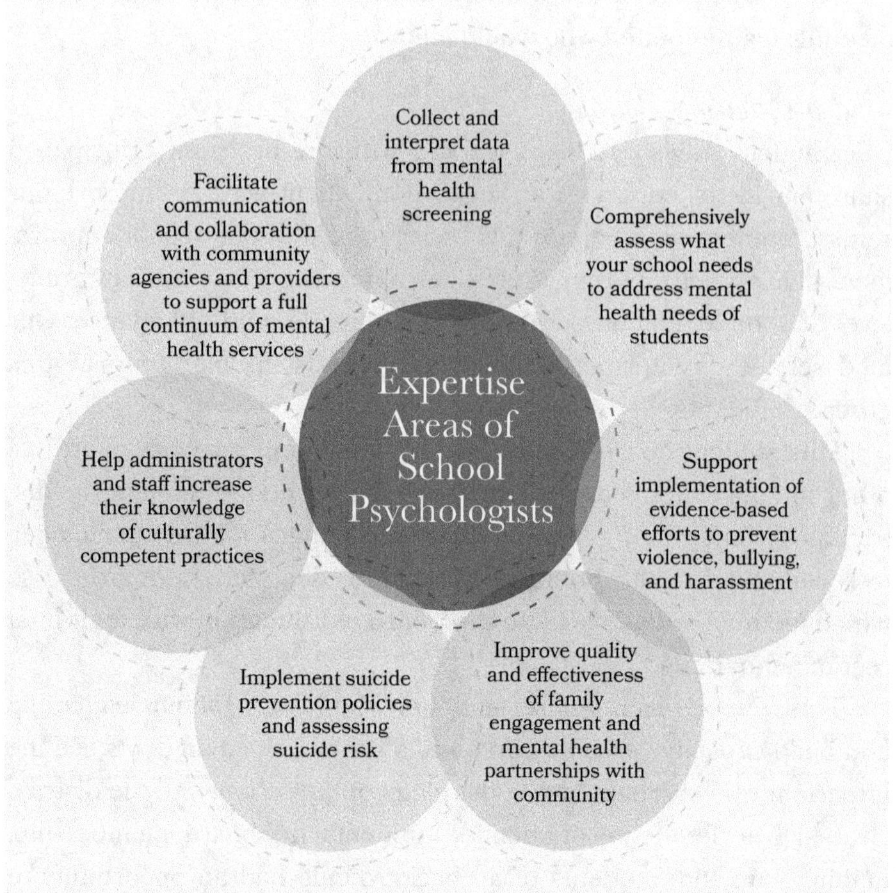

Source: NASP, "ESSA School Climate for School Psychologists," https://www.naspon-line.org/x36067.xml

the various skills and capacities a person with a degree or a certificate in school psychology brings to the table.

Figure 6.5 illustrates the numerous competencies of school psychologists. They can conduct individual or schoolwide mental health screening and interpret the data. They can provide expertise when your school is forming a response to a bullying incident and can help you construct anti-bullying policies and programs. School psychologists have training regarding suicide prevention and assessing suicide risk. They can provide valuable information about culturally competent practices and help your school implement them. In any situation where the school is working with others, whether they are families of students or community agencies, a school psychologist can facilitate good communication that leads to stronger relationships.

But that's not all school psychologists can do. They can also help a school adjust how curriculum is delivered so students hit a particular target. For example, if a particular grade is struggling with the math curriculum, a school psychologist can look at the data to identify the problem and make suggestions about how to change classroom delivery in ways that students can process more easily.[8]

The Every Student Succeeds Act (ESSA) authorizes funding for services school psychologists provide under Titles I, II, and IV. Title IV, Part A requires schools to spend at least 20 percent of Student Support and Academic Enhancement Grants for comprehensive school mental and behavioral health service delivery systems, trauma-informed policies and practices, bullying and harassment prevention, social-emotional learning, improving school safety and school climate, mental health first aid training, and professional development activities.

Figure 6.6 lists the mental and behavioral health services school psychologists provide that can be funded with ESSA money.

As I am writing this book, emergency funds to support students' transitions back to classrooms after the pandemic have been available for two years: the Elementary and Secondary School Fund (ESSER) and the Governor's Emergency Education Relief Fund (GEER). Both of these emergency funds can be used to pay for services school psychologists provide.

Figure 6.6. *Comprehensive mental and behavioral health services funded under ESSA*

TIER 1: UNIVERSAL SERVICES

- Universal screening for academic, behavioral, and emotional barriers to learning.
- Integration of social-emotional learning into the curriculum.
- Provision of staff development related to identification of mental health concerns.
- Reinforcement of a behavior that contributes to a positive school environment.

TIER 2: TARGETED SERVICES

- Assessment of suicide risk and suicide threats.
- Provision of individual and group counseling.
- Provision of skill building groups.
- Development and monitoring of behavior intervention plan.
- Consultation with teachers and/or families regarding students' mental health and behavioral problems.

TIER 3: INTENSIVE SERVICES

- Direct therapeutic services to all students in need.
- Psychological assessment of social, emotional, and behavioral problems.
- Crisis intervention.
- Development of crisis response plans with administration and staff.

Source: NASP, "ESSA Mental and Behavioral Health Services for Decision-Makers," https://www.nasponline.org/research-and-policy/policy-priorities/relevant-law/the-every-student-succeeds-act/essa-implementation-resources/essa-mental-and-behavioral-health-services-for-decision-makers

What Administrators Can Do to Address the Shortage of School Psychologists

School psychologists are essential staff for schools that provide comprehensive mental health supports to students. A full-time school psychologist who meets National Certification of School Psychologists (NCSP) standards is the ideal. However, there is a national shortage of school psychologists in the United States. The problem is two-fold: (1) not enough people are graduating with national certification as school psychologists; and (2) many districts do not pay school psychologists at a rate commensurate with their skill.

The shortage is severe. In 2021, there were 57,110 school psychologists nationwide and over 128,000 public and private primary and secondary schools.[9] The National Association of School Psychologists (NASP) recommends a ratio of 500 students to each school psychologist, but in many states the ratio is three or four times that (or more). (See a map of state shortages on the NASP's State Shortages Data Dashboard, https://www.nasponline.org/about-school-psychology/state-shortages-data-dashboard) The result is overworked school psychologists, to the point where some would like to leave the profession. A recent national survey of school psychologists found that 16 percent want to leave the profession after five years because of overwork. Half of that group said they wanted to leave because of coercive interactions with administrators.[10] Each school psychologist is a precious resource that contributes to the well-being of the next generation. We can't afford to lose any of them.

As an administrator, you can take steps on several levels to advocate for more school psychologists and to use practices that will retain practicing school psychologists.

1. Encourage your state principals' association to work with state legislators and your state governor to provide salary stipends to achieve NSCP parity. Teachers and administrators who meet the National Board for Professional Teaching Standards (NBPTS) are typically awarded a salary stipend from state or district funds. The position of the NASP is that school psychologists who meet the standards of NCSP should also have stipends that raise their salaries to levels comparable to those of administrators. For more about this issue, see "Advocating for a Salary Stipend for Nationally Certified School Psychologists (NCSP)," https://www.nasponline.org/research-and-policy/advocacy/ncsp-parity. That page is written for school psychologists, but it has information and links school principals can use to participate in this advocacy.

2. Break down the list of components of a comprehensive mental health support system in Figure 6.6 into tasks mental health professionals must do and tasks you can do as a school, then work with local agencies to hire psychologists to provide the services only a mental health professional is qualified to do. The NASP has prepared several PDFs to guide you in these partnerships: "Effective School-Community Partnerships to Support School Mental Health"; "Nine Elements of Effective School Community Partnerships to Address Student Mental Health, Physical Health, and Overall Wellness" (links to these two sites available at https://apps.nasponline.org/search-results.aspx?q=community); and "Considerations for Contract Services in School Psychology" (link available at https://apps.nasponline.org/search-results.aspx?q=contract).

3. If your school is fortunate enough to have a school psychologist, work closely with them to ensure that their work-

load is doable. Always interact with them with respect and acknowledge their contributions to the welfare of your students. Do not make demands: those types of interactions are a primary reason that certified school psychologists leave the profession.

4. Contact colleges and universities in your state that grant degrees in school psychology to learn how you can support them. What can school administrators do to increase the number of students who pursue school psychology as a career? How can school administrators support the efforts of school psychologists with state and national legislators? What kinds of partnerships can you form with degree-granting programs, departments, and schools that would benefit them? (See Appendix C for a list of colleges and universities by state.)

5. Learn what steps you can take to get your school approved for hosting internships for school psychologists. Individuals who graduate with a degree in school psychology must complete 1,200 hours of internship. Most of those hours involve providing direct services to children and families. Find out from your local college or university that grants school psychologist degrees if it is feasible for your school to become an approved site.

Resource List

Richard DuFour, Rebecca DuFour, Robert Eaker, and Gayle Karhanek, *Whatever It Takes: How Professional Learning Communities Respond When Kids Don't Learn* (Solution Tree, 2004).

Written in th e era of No Child Left Behind and a growing focus on standardized testing, this book by the founders of the concept of professional learning communities describes how teams can help students succeed academically. It is largely based on a case study from Adlai Stevenson High School in Chicago. You won't find content about social-emotional learning, student mental health, or increasing equity in this book. What you *will* find is an excellent in-depth exploration of how a team can respond when a student is struggling to learn. One of the strengths of the book is the concept of a "pyramid of interventions" teams can use to assist students. Another strength is its attention to the concept of collective responses to challenges. This approach draws attention to the knowledge and experience of each member of school staff and lends itself well to collaborative solution-seeking. The professional learning community is a model leaders can build on to serve the specific needs of their school.

Richard DuFour, Rebecca DuFour, Robert Eaker, Thomas W. Many, and Mike Mattos, *Learning by Doing: A Handbook for Professional Learning Communities at Work,* 3rd ed. (Solution Tree, 2016).

This manual offers concrete steps schools can take to transition to a PLC model. The third edition includes two new chapters, one on how teams can develop common assessment strategies and another on hiring, orienting, and retaining staff members for your PLC. It offers information about avoiding common mistakes related to the PLC process, suggestions for developing a focus on learning deeper knowledge (as opposed to simple information recall), and strategies for addressing conflict within a PLC. A companion book, *Concise Answers to Frequently Asked Questions about Professional Learning Communities at Work,* provides readers with quick answers to help them move beyond specific problems in PLC implementation.

Sax Institute, *School-Based Prevention and Early Intervention for Student Mental Health and Wellbeing* (Sax Institute, 2020).

This list of 74 school-based mental health prevention and early intervention programs implemented in Australian schools provides information about which ones were effective and which characteristics drove effectiveness and sustainability. The rigorous, evidence-based analysis of programs may help leaders and their community allies design programs to serve the mental health needs of students. The programs are divided into five categories: anxiety and depression, self-injury and suicide, autism spectrum disorder, attention deficit hyperactivity disorder and conduct problems, body image problems and eating disorders, and general programs.

Ron Berger and Ann Vilen, *We Are Crew: A Teamwork Approach to School Culture* (EL Education, 2021).

"We believe that addressing the inequities inherent in school structures, conditions, and outcomes is the greatest educational priority of our time. For that reason, creating a culture of Crew that brings historically underserved students, regardless of background or identity, into the circle of belonging is imperative." This is the starting point for *We Are Crew,* a guide to developing a school culture that affirms diverse identities, fosters belonging, and centers relationships based on trust. The book introduces EL Education's Character Framework, a three-dimensional vision of student achievement based on mastery of knowledge and skills, character development, and high-quality student work. These three vectors of achievement are developed in the framework of crews, or small advisory groups of peers and staff that meet daily for mutual support and accountability. Chapters walk schools through creating a culture of crew, building staff crew, creating a crew structure, helping students become effective learners through crew, helping students become ethical people through crew, helping students contribute to a better world through crew, preparing students for college and careers through crew, and improving crew across the school. Chapters are supported with a series of open-access videos and downloadable documents.

Kirleen Neely, Kimberley Orsten Hooge, Tom Thelen, and Elliott Kagan, *Mental Health 101 for Teens: The Practical Guide to Mental Health, Self-Esteem, and Emotional Intelligence,* 3rd ed. (Character Programs, 2022).

Mental Health 101 for Teens is a whole-school training program that includes school assemblies, parent programs, teacher trainings and a whole-school curriculum for middle and high school students. The book helps teens distinguish between temporary feelings of anxiety or depression and longer forms of mental illness, teaches positive behaviors and mental well-being skills, teaches prevention of at-risk and self-destructive behaviors, shows students how to get support by talking to a trusted adult, and shows students how to get help in a mental health crisis. This research-based resource can be taught as a Tier 1 class for middle school and high school students. A website for the book (mentalhealth101.org) offers a deep bench of resources for schools, including curriculum, virtual and/or in-person live trainings of various lengths to help students cope with depression and anxiety, and an interview with lead author Tom Thelen.

7

New Rules, New Roles: Principal Mental Health in a Post-Covid School

Finding ways to effectively support our leaders through increasing levels of professional support, self-efficacy, and connectedness is critical to reducing compassion fatigue and turnover.

—Meg Stomski, et al., "Finding Resilience during the
COVID-19 Pandemic: Perspectives from School Leaders"

What does the job description for a school principal look like in 2023? A lot has changed since the beginning of this century. For most of the twentieth century, principals were taught that one of the most import-ant aspects of their job was managing the school building. Since the pandemic, principals have been getting conflicting messages from var-ious places about what they are supposed to be doing. The University of North Carolina's School of Education website says that "principals' effects are largely indirect, stemming from their work to hire and develop teachers and in creating conditions for sound learning."[1] Another source concurs that instructional leadership is where principals should be focusing: "The key role of school administrators should be instructional leadership in the current era of accountability."[2] An article on the Frontiers in Education website argues that principals should look at the changing world around us and then "consistently express the skills . . . and capabilities . . . society wants students to have." The authors argue that today's society needs students who are adaptable, creative, collaborative, and communicative and show initiative and that principals need to model these qualities "to a high degree."[3] An article on the Edutopia website said that principals need to "transform . . . schools into community learning centers that are led and valued by students, families, and the communities they serve." A watchdog group that monitors state spending to make sure it's used efficiently found that effective principals develop strong relationships with students and their families; are very engaged in classrooms, sometimes even teaching classes; create a collaborative culture for teachers; are key contributors to curriculum development; and "prioritize becoming a hub for the community."[5] Each of these domains is a tall order to master, and it's no wonder that school principals are feeling stressed and pressured.

There is reason to doubt that this conflicting advice is welcome. Several recent surveys found strong evidence that school principals are struggling. In 2021, the National Association of Secondary School Principals (NASSP) published the results of a new survey of principals and students. Three-quarters of principals reported that they felt that they needed a great deal of support for their mental health, but only just over half had sought help. Principals reported overwhelming mental health needs for both themselves and their students, poor work-life balance, poor state and federal responses to their needs, staffing shortages, and a mismatch between what they did each week and how they would like to allocate their time.[6] Another 2022 survey found that 85% of principal respondents were frequently experiencing job-related stress and 48% were burned out.[7] The NASSP report prominently featured a quote from an Indiana principal that expressed the feelings of many principals across the country: "Principals in every state are facing enormous challenges resulting in significant stress with no end in sight. The survey results make clear that while we love working with students and teachers, our conditions are unsustainable and if left unaddressed, could result in principal shortages that will be difficult to overcome."[8]

None of this will be news to you. If you are a principal, you are leading a school through what one education analyst speculates may be "the most difficult [years] in the history of U.S. education."[9] Tabari Wallace, an advisor to the North Carolina Department of Public Instruction, said that in the wake of the pandemic, "the principals have been the glue that has kept education together. The reason principal mental health is so concerning today is principals pour into the vessels of everyone else—students, teachers, central office staff. But who is meeting the needs of the principal?"[10] Resilience has become a more important issue than it has ever been before for school principals. But how can principals find resilience when they are pushed to the limits of what they can do every day?

One component of resilience is cultivating strong relationships with the people around you. A majority of the principals who responded to the 2022 NASSP survey said that they wished they could spend more time with students, more time supporting teachers, and more time observing classrooms. Instead, they found themselves devoting significant chunks of time every week to administrative paperwork and meetings.[11]

I do not pretend to have all the answers for principals who are coping with unprecedented political and social conditions. What I can tell you is the leadership you show now will have a deeper impact than it ever has before. And I can tell you about my experience with leading a school with over 75 percent of students experiencing poverty and trauma.

I was fortunate to participate in the Wallace Foundation School Administration Manager (SAM) Project in my first two years as principal at Fall Ridge. This project tracked how principals spent their time and analyzed that data. It encouraged principals to delegate some tasks to other people in the building—either a full-time school administration manager or people who had skills in the delegated area—so the principal could spend more time on instructional leadership. The principals who participated in the project received mentoring in time management and delegation for a year.

During the years I was participating, the project found that principals increased the time they devoted to instructional leadership tasks (such as observation and walk-throughs and work with students) by an average of five hours each week. They gained this time by decreasing the number of minutes they spent each day on discipline, student supervision, managing non-teaching staff, managing school facilities, and interacting with parents.[12] These tasks were delegated to others.

Although the ultimate goal of the project was creating more time for principals for instructional leadership, there was a lack of consensus among my fellow project participants about what instructional leadership meant. Some said it meant supporting teachers, some said it meant being more visible in the school, some said it meant coaching teachers, some said they would like to create collaborative relationships with teachers, and others felt that an instructional leader was the "lead teacher."[13]

I was very clear about my definition of instructional leadership. Everything I did in my job as principal centered on building relationships of trust. For me, that meant trusting the knowledge and experience of my staff. Collectively, they had many years of wisdom about what worked and what didn't. That is not to say that they knew everything, and we were certainly in an unprecedented situation in our school in terms of trauma and poverty. So, for me, leadership in instruction meant listening to my staff about what they felt they needed in order to teach effectively.

The team structure worked very well for collecting that information and conveying it to the Building Leadership Team. Each grade had five to eight teams. Each leader from that team reported their needs to an all-grade meeting of team leaders. Information from that meeting would be carried to the Building Leadership Team by the team leader representative for that grade.

When I learned of an instructional need, I would reach into my local and interstate networks of principal colleagues to hear how they had responded to the particular issue our school was struggling with. I would listen to them to identify the best person to come to our school and provide guidance and mentoring based on their experience with what worked. I rarely turned to packages sold by companies. I wanted help for our teachers that I knew would work for our school.

For example, one year my staff reported that students were having trouble with reading comprehension and writing. I turned to the colleagues in my network and asked who else was having this difficulty at their school. Who did they know who was an expert about teaching writing? What was their experience with that person? Did their methods work? Were they effective?

The name that kept coming up was Kristina Smekens. My colleagues could vouch for the effectiveness of the professional development she offered teachers. I spoke at length with Kristina before bringing her to Fall Ridge to make sure that she would bring what our teachers needed. I didn't want "sit and get" professional development. I wanted our teachers to leave their workshop with her with concrete actions they could do.

Kristina was just right for Fall Ridge teachers. I hired floating substitutes the day she came so teachers could watch her. She showed our teachers a lesson and discussed the pedagogical concepts behind it. Then she went into a classroom and taught the lesson while teachers observed. Afterward, they talked with her and asked questions and she gave them the lesson supplies they needed. Then she came a second time, this time to watch a Fall Ridge teacher teach the lesson and provide additional mentorship and guidance. We had developed a model lesson that all the teachers were using. She provided feedback on that lesson and many suggestions about things to try.[14]

This kind of professional development was built from the ground up in several ways. First, the request came from the teachers. They were the ones who decided what they needed and passed the request up through the team structure to my desk. Second, the mentorship Kristina provided was based on experiences in the classroom. Kristina knew her pedagogy worked and had many suggestions about how to tweak it to meet the needs of many types of students. Third, Kristina offered in-person dialogue with teachers. Because of that, both sides were confident that what she offered was tailored to meet the specific needs of our students.

That is one kind of instructional leadership—listening to what teachers want and making sure that what you offer will meet their needs. Reaching for easy-to-acquire, pre-packaged solutions may not be right for your school. You need to lead from the ground up.

A second kind of instructional leadership is based on a principal's observations about a gap in knowledge or a need to adjust to new circumstances. An example of that is the exercise I mentioned in Chapter 4 about how teachers perceived Fall Ridge students. I had proposed that we use Eric Jensen's book *Teaching with Poverty in Mind* as the basis for a professional development session. I heard some pushback from staff members who felt that they didn't need that kind of development. After all, they had been teaching poor kids for years. But when they put their composite images of students on the wall and realized that everything they had said about the students they were teaching was negative, they realized that yes, they did need some more education about how poverty affects education.

Both kinds of leadership are based on open, trusting relationships with staff. My staff knew I trusted them and respected their experience. They knew that if they came to me with a request, I would say yes more often than not. One year an eighth-grade science class got very excited about their lessons about cell biology. One student said, "Hey, wouldn't it be great if we could build a giant cell and have the school come and see it?" When their teacher told me about this, I said, "Sure, why not? Just make sure they don't change any permanent infrastructure." The school custodian helped them find scraps of building materials and they turned their classroom into a giant cell. There were several stations in the room where students had prepared presentations about a particular aspect of cell biology. Students from other classes came to tour the giant cell. Everybody loved it, and the students and their teacher learned that I welcomed their ideas.

My relationship-centered approach to my job meant that I allocated my time differently from many of my colleagues. This was possible because of the team structure I created at Fall Ridge. Figure 7.1 shows how I allocated time in a typical work week, compared to the time spent by Ontario principals in a 2015 study. You can see from this table that the areas where I spent the largest chunks of time involved face-to-face interactions with students and staff.

The Ontario principals spent more time on traditional management tasks, such as internal school management, personnel, budget/office needs, district meetings, and student discipline than I did. I delegated many of those tasks to my secretary, my assistant principal, and the Building Leadership Team (although I did have to attend the district meetings). My secretary did the time-consuming task of managing the budget and each team managed the portion of the budget allocated to them. Our guidance counselor monitored attendance data.

Grade-Level Teams also did work that took some of the weight off my shoulders. They were the first to intervene when a student was having an attendance issue, for example. That student's case would move up through the layers of the team structure before I became involved. But when an attendance case reached the Building Leadership Intervention Team, I attended each meeting.

Figure 7.1. *Principal Time Allocation (hours per week)*

Area or Activity	Me	Ontario Principals
Classroom walk-throughs/observations/evaluations	8.0	3.1
Preventive work with students (trauma, SEL, bullying, academics, attendance)	7.0	0.0
Student discipline	5.0	7.6
Visibility (walking hallways, visiting lunchroom)	5.0	5.8
Student-related activities	5.0	5.2
Curriculum and instructional leadership	5.0	5.0
District meetings	4.0	5.4
Safety/maintenance/health	4.0	3.3
Building meetings	4.0	0.0
Professional development for staff	4.0	0.0
Parent meetings	3.0	5.6
Student transportation	2.0	1.2
Budget/office needs	1.5	1.8
Internal school management[1]	3.0	7.5
Principal's professional development	0.0	2.0
Personnel	0.0	5.6
	60.5[15]	59.1

Source: Author's personal data; Ontario data from Katina Pollock, Fei Wang, and David Cameron Hauseman, "Complexity and Volume: An Inquiry into Factors that Drive Principals' Work," *Societies* 5 (2015): 549.

[1] For the Ontario principals, this involved managing the calendar, office management, memos, the newsletter, the website, and so forth. For me, it included writing a newsletter and communicating with staff.

What Do We Know about What Makes an Effective Principal?

In 2021, the Wallace Foundation released a report that synthesized two decades of research on what principals do and what makes them effective. The report grouped principals' skill sets into three broad categories: instructional leadership, relationships with people, and managing the organization. The report's summary of the literature on instructional leadership found that effective instructional leaders provide constructive, actionable feedback to teachers and offer "high-quality professional development opportunities" to their staff.[16] In the domain of relationships, research shows that effective principals create a caring environment; communicate effectively with teachers, students, and families; cultivate trust with students and teachers; offer proactive support to new teachers; and "are committed to the success of both novice and veteran teachers."[17] Organization management includes the more traditional skills of managing budgets and resources and developing a safe school environment; research shows that prioritization of these skills predicts "higher student achievement growth, teacher satisfaction, and parent ratings of the school." Data-use skills have emerged as important for making decisions across several domains of a principal's job. Finally, setting goals and thinking strategically about how to use resources to meet those goals has been identified as an important component of managing a school.[18]

Plugging the time allocation data from me in 2008–2012 and from the Ontario principals in 2015 into the three main skill categories the Wallace Foundation has identified shows a significant difference in prioritization (see Figure 7.2).

This table clearly shows the impact of delegating management tasks. I was able to devote almost 10 hours more to instructional leadership than the Ontario principals because I could rely on other staff to handle public relations, collecting and analyzing data, managing the budget, and most of the work of maintaining a safe school environment.

Figure 7.2. *My allocation of time and Ontario principals' allocation of time organized according to the Wellman Foundation categories of effective principal leadership (hours per week)*

	Me	Ontario Principals
Instructional Leadership		
District meetings	4.0	5.4
Building meetings	4.0	0.0
Classroom walk-throughs/observations/evaluations	8.0	3.1
Professional development: building and personal	4.0	0.0
Principal's professional development	0.0	2.0
Curriculum and instructional leadership	5.0	5.0
	25.0	15.5
Relationships		
Personnel	0.0	5.6
Communications	3.0	0.0
Visibility and lunchroom duty	5.0	5.8
Student discipline	5.0	7.6
Student-related activities	5.0	5.2
Student meetings: (trauma, SEL, bullying, academic, attendance)	7.0	0.0
Parent meetings	3.0	5.6
Student transportation	2.0	1.2
	30.0	31.0
Building Management		
Budget/office needs	1.5	1.8
Safety/maintenance/health	4.0	3.3
Internal school management	0.0	7.5
	5.5	12.6
Totals	**60.5**	**59.1**

Our school resource officer, the guidance counselor, my secretary, the school custodian, and the Building Leadership Team took on many of the traditional management tasks that in the twentieth century occupied the lion's share of a principal's time. That is not to say that I opted out of those tasks completely. I still did safety checks every day. I had my eye on the budget. I reviewed data frequently. But I relied on staff in my building to do most of this work.

Delegation enabled me to devote more of my time to building and strengthening relationships with students, staff, and families. Those relationships were what created an environment that felt so emotionally safe to students that they would come to school when everything in their lives would have predicted chronic absenteeism. They came to school because that is where they felt good, like they were part of a family that cared about them.

The caring relationships I modeled became the norm among students and between teachers and students. Everyone realized that their day went better when they had warm bonds of trust and caring with each other. Those bonds created an environment that was conducive to learning, that encouraged students to propose ideas like converting their classroom to a giant cell so they could share what they had learned, that ensured that no student fell through the cracks because of mental health issues.

I encountered many situations in my time at Fall Ridge that I never could have imagined when I was training to be a principal. Seven students in my school were registered sex offenders. Another student was on probation and came to school with an ankle bracelet. Students came to school in wet clothes because they had washed them by hand and didn't realize how long it would take them to dry. Students came to school in the winter wearing just a sweater or a light fall jacket; several teachers made a project of buying winter coats at thrift stores so they could give them to students who needed them. I talked with many parents who were close to the edge because of the tremendous pressure they were under. I talked to some who had gone over the edge, and we had to work with the Department of Children and Family Ser-vices to get their children rehomed. I promised a dying mother I would see that her girls went to college (and they did). I made home visits to comfort grieving parents after students had been killed in car accidents (and one time because a boy had been hit by a train). I heard stories of frequent gunfire related to gangs in the neighborhoods my students lived in. I supported a grieving 14-year-old twin whose brother had died. Being a school principal means seeing life in its rawest, harshest form some days. If you don't have a foundation of strong relationships, if peo-ple don't know if they can trust you, you will have many uncomfortable moments as you face situations that are dire or traumatic.

That is why I made relationships the heart of my work as a princi-pal. It is why almost every interaction I had with a student was filtered through the lens of social-emotional learning the two rules teach. It is why nearly every hour I spent on instructional leadership was also about relationships—building trust, building capacity in others, building students and their teachers up, looking for and finding the best situa-tion for each student and each teacher.

Building Capacity through Delegation

In addition to the support from teams, we had professionals in our build-ing who focused on specific aspects of the work we did. The dean of stu-dents handled the discipline of the building. Our school social worker and our school psychologist supported the behavioral (social-emotional) aspects of discipline, working with the dean. My assistant principal helped me oversee curriculum and instruction.

My head secretary handled the management of the building by com-pleting the newsletter, compiling daily announcements, managing our website, managing the substitutes, keeping track of building keys, keep-ing track of our building financials, and determining who could get to see me. (Although she had instructions to always let a student in whenever they asked to see me.) She also helped me manage my emails. I looked at each one I got and triaged them. Some I responded to myself, but most got forwarded to her with a short note about how I wanted to respond. She then responded on my behalf.

The guidance office staff (a guidance counselor and one support staff) managed student schedules and student records. They analyzed their data in ways that revealed (for example) trends and possible gaps in our curriculum so I could determine what kind of support students and teachers needed. Staff from this office also worked to support the intervention team.

The attendance office worked directly with the truancy officer. They also maintained a database of family contacts that included more than one name for each student.

I also worked to build capacity with my staff. For example, we had one teacher who had taught physical education and health classes for years. No one had ever asked her to do anything beyond that. I asked her if she would be interested in putting together a student and teacher workshop day on health and wellness. She was delighted and told me that she had many ideas about that topic. She put together a committee of faculty colleagues and together they contacted community people who came to Fall Ridge and delivered excellent content for both students and teachers on health and wellness.

When I hired faculty for the Building Leadership Team, I looked for skills that could be developed further on that team in the domains of data management, public relations, curriculum development, team leadership, or communication with colleagues. Activities that might have been simply areas of interest or "something I guess I'm good at" became well-developed skills that could transfer to other areas of professional development or community activities. Often I was able to facilitate greater skill development for Building Leadership Team members through training or courses.

I was always transparent when I discussed major decisions for our building with the Building Leadership Team. I shared all of the data I had with them. Everyone had the same information and we collectively decided how to move forward. This open collaboration added layers of trust to our relationships with each other. Sometimes we had to make decisions before we had all the information we needed from the district. But because of our deep trust in one another, we had confidence that we could adjust our decisions as more information came in. We worked together to solve challenges using data and our collective experience as our guides. I didn't go into meetings with a preconceived idea of how our decisions should go. I trusted that leadership team to bring their wisdom and experience to our conversations and we moved forward based on a common sense of where we needed to go based on our mission and our needs.

This model is called *distributed leadership*. One researcher defines the role of the administrator in a distributed leadership model as "primarily about enhancing the skills and knowledge of people in the organization, creating a common culture of expectations around the use of those skills and knowledge, holding various pieces of the organization together in a productive relationship with each other, and holding individuals accountable for their contributions to the collective result."[19] Other research shows that when this model is implemented "planfully" (that is, not spontaneously or with misalignments), it contributes to a positive school environment, increases student motivation to learn, and leads to greater teacher effectiveness and empowerment.[20]

Delegating traditional building management tasks and distributing decision-making about school policies and practices using a collaborative team approach with faculty can help principals cope with the many and increasing demands on their time and attention. These strategies may lead to daily schedules that enable administrators to devote more time to the tasks that require their specialized knowledge and skills so they can provide leadership in the domains where their schools need them most.

Resilience Skills for Principals

The Covid-19 pandemic has pushed many principals to the brink of what they can cope with. In addition to pushback from parents about Covid-related safety policies, principals are in the crosshairs of public attacks on education about race. Many are facing budget cuts that threaten their ability to deliver educational equity to all students. Each day since schools reopened after the Covid lockdown, principals have faced unpredictable, unprecedented challenges and emergencies. One principal in Maine summarized her experience in 2022:

> The best way to describe it is walking up to the edge of a cliff, with one foot solidly placed on the ground and the other foot ready to go over the edge. . . . As an admin, it's not uncommon to do a 12- or 14-hour day under normal circumstances. Throw in a pandemic, and you're just so tired. My brain never got the opportunity to shut down, recharge. We're still in that mode, even though we're hopeful next school year will be different.[21]

In addition to the increased workload related to the pandemic, most principals of color have experienced racism. In 2022, over 60 percent of principals of color reported that families of students harassed them online or in person because of their race or ethnicity, that they experienced verbal or nonverbal microaggressions from families of students, and that family members acted uncomfortable around them because of their race or ethnicity. They also experienced racism from their supervisors; over 50 percent reported that their supervisors held them to different standards or expected them to perform additional tasks because of their race or ethnicity.[22] Principals of all racial and ethnic backgrounds reported that exposure to school violence and harassment about Covid-19 safety policies at their school had contributed to burnout, job stress, depression, or the feeling that they were not doing well.[23]

These challenges have had a devastating impact on the mental health of school principals.[24] Principal morale is so low that a significant proportion is planning to leave the profession within the next five years. Over a third (38%) of the respondents to the NASSP survey were planning to leave their jobs within the next three years.[25] Over a quarter (28%) were planning to leave the field of education altogether.[26] One study found that the top reasons principals gave for considering such a drastic move were not enough time for instructional leadership; not enough teachers, teaching assistants, paraprofessionals, or school counselors; and too many hours in the work week.[27]

Researchers at the 21st Century California School Leadership Academy (21CSLA) at UC Berkeley have been surveying California principals since the spring of 2021 in order to identify the factors that support resilience during the pandemic. Survey results from the first year of the study showed that a high sense of self-efficacy—a principal's belief that they were taking the actions that were needed to produce improvements in their school—and a strong feeling of connectedness to their school and their district were associated with lower levels of compassion fatigue, which the study defined as "behaviors and emotions resulting from being exposed to and knowing about a traumatizing event experienced by others and the stress resulting from wanting to help a traumatized or suffering person."[28] Another finding of the survey was that "professional circumstances such as increased networks and support may contribute to the resilience of some principals."[29]

In the second wave of the study, they focused on the strategies principals were using to build resilience. Almost half of the respondents had turned to individual strategies such as physical activity, maintaining physical and psychological well-being, maintaining clear work/life boundaries, focusing on positive thinking, and doing things that brought them joy (e.g., hobbies). Almost 40 percent relied on connections to social and professional networks. One respondent said, "Finding a bit of time to call, email, laugh, and joke about work and life helps bring perspective. Without these colleagues who are going through what can only be called uncharted waters I would consider walking away." Others reported that role efficacy and the sense that their administrative team was working together to move their school forward sustained them. Some said that their spiritual and moral beliefs were sources of resilience for them. In a webinar titled "Principal Resilience" associated with the study, researchers and participants discussed the benefits principals derived from setting strong work-life boundaries (e.g., committing to going home at 5 p.m. every day, turning off the phone while at home), such as increased energy and a greater ability to cope with unexpected setbacks. Other topics included coping with the unpredictability of stressors principals were experiencing, the benefits of focusing on a domain of responsibility a principal could control, being more open about not knowing answers in meetings with colleagues and asking for help to find answers together, and the need for a multitiered system of support for principals.[30]

It may seem counterintuitive to talk about looking for joy when you're under great stress. But Ingrid Fetell Lee argues that it can be a major strategy for carrying you through a hard time. She contrasts joy with happiness, which she defines as an overall feeling of well-being over time. Joy, Lee says, is that pop of excitement that happens in the moment when you see or hear or feel or touch something that makes you feel like jumping up and down. She says that "as a culture we are obsessed with the pursuit of happiness, but in the process, we kind of overlooked joy." She went on a quest to learn where joy comes from, talking to many people and looking at many cultures.

What she learned is that there are patterns to the things that bring people joy that transcend age, culture, gender, politics, or any other quality. Examples are:

- Round things (polka dots, spinning tops, Ferris wheels)
- Pops of bright color (an ice cream cone with sprinkles, bright-colored fabric or yarn, a new box of crayons, Lego® blocks)
- Symmetrical shapes (a mosaic floor, a series of identical arches on a building, a starfish, a sunflower, a pieced quilt)
- A sense of abundance and multiplicity (a jar of colored marbles, a ball pit for kids, a basket of peaches)
- A feeling of lightness or elevation (bubbles, dandelion seeds floating in the air, fireworks, a hot air balloon, a fluffy cloud)

We can find joy through synchrony with others too. Neuroscientists have found that when people play musical instruments together or sing together, their brain activity becomes synchronized and their heartbeats align. These physiological responses can lead to prosocial behaviors, for example being more likely to help a partner or make a sacrifice for the good of a group. Even sitting in chairs and rocking together at the same tempo can lead a group to perform better on a collaborative task.

Lee says that "deep within us, we all have this impulse to seek out joy in our surroundings. And we have it for a reason. Joy isn't some superfluous extra. It's directly connected to our fundamental instinct for survival." So look for joy in your life. String moments of joy together on an imaginary cord that can surround you. Return in your memory to moments when you were joyful. You will be surprised about how much moments of joy can sustain you in times of stress.

Source: Ingrid Fetell Lee, "Where Joy Hides and How to Find It," Ted Talk, 2018, https://www.ted.com/talks/ingrid_fetell_lee_where_joy_hides_and_how_to_find_it; Ingrid Fetell Lee, *Joyful: The Surprising Power of Ordinary Things to Create Extraordinary Happiness* (Little, Brown Spark, 2018), 244. Download Lee's "The Joyspotter's Guide" through a link on the Ted Talk page.

A particularly beneficial resilience resource that emerged from the 21CLSA study is working one-on-one with a coach or mentor on work-life balance. The principals who participated in the 21CLSA study were fortunate to have access to a coach who worked with them each week. Participants found that their local and extralocal professional networks weren't enough. One coach reported that a principal told her, "Yes, she has some network in her district, but those people are drowning in work too. . . . They want to help each other, but the fact is there's not going to be another principal that's going to sit down with her for an hour each week uninterrupted prepared to take her through this process of reflection [about building resilience]."[31] A member of the research team noted that a finding of the study was that "good coaches will help people do some of the things that [principals] reported as positive protective factors in our study."[32]

Developing resilience skills such as self-care, asking for help, and having a good work-life balance isn't easy. These are complex skills that don't develop overnight. They require attention and daily follow-through. Most people need support to develop and strengthen them. This is where district support for principal wellness can have a large impact. One participant in the 21CSLA study said, "Our district has organized administrators and has been working through Elena Aguilar's book *Onward*. We do the work and then plan out how to share what we do with our staff. This has helped put things into perspective as well as helped our staff develop resilience."[33] (See Appendix 3 for more information on Elena Aguilar's books on building resilience for educators.) Shane Safir, writing for the NASSP, says, "We need to turn our notions of accountability upside down and begin to position states and districts as accountable to principals, teachers, students, and the community rather than the other way around. One principal at our meeting observed that he has never once been asked by a district leader, 'What can we do to better support you in leading your school?' This simple shift from telling and issuing mandates to inquiring and listening for insight would be monumental." She argues that "districts and states need to build the infrastructure for robust, quality coaching models for principals."[34] Mentors for early-career principals and coaches for mid- and later-career administrators can help school leaders identify what kind of principal they want to be, build resilience skills, and develop the work-life balance that so many principals need in order to protect their mental health.

Resource List

Brian K. Creasman, *Prioritizing Health and Well-Being: Self-Care as a Leadership Strategy for School Leaders* (Rowman & Littlefield, 2022).

In a foreword to this book, American Association of School Superintendents executive director Daniel Domenech writes, "If there is one thing that is certain in a world full of unpleasantness and uncertainties like we find ourselves in today, it's that every school-system leader, administrator, building leader, lead teacher, or anyone associated with educating our children needs to raise the bar when it comes to self-care." Author Brian Creasman writes that learning self-care is essential for a sustainable pace of work, noting that many school leaders are leaving their jobs because of burnout and that many who reach retirement live constricted lives because of poor health after carrying a workload that was too heavy for decades. Learning self-care is not easy for school leaders because they are steeped in the heroic leader model. This book shows education leaders how to learn new ways in 22 easily digestible chapters that guide readers through a particular aspect of self-care. Each chapter offers practical strategies, voices from the field, and key takeaways. Although this book is written for district superintendents, the information is valuable for every educator and administrator.

John A. DeFlaminis, Mustafa Abdul-Jabbar, and Eric Yoak, *Distributed Leadership in Schools: A Practical Guide for Learning and Improvement* (Taylor and Francis, 2016).

Distributed Leadership in Schools is a measured reflection on the Annenberg Distributed Leadership Project, a study that helped schools introduce distributed leadership in 2006–2010. The book combines theory with experience-based learning. It presents distributed leadership as the antidote to the "heroic leader" model that has influenced principal training for many years. Chapters lay out the distributed leadership model; describe how to design a distributed leadership system in a school; discuss curriculum, instruction, and coaching in a distributed leadership program; describe how to build distributed leadership teams; and offer an evidence-based model of leadership behaviors that promote trust in schools. The book has three useful appendices: a teacher-leader interview form, an action planning format, and a checklist for schools moving to a distributed leadership structure. Readers who are interested in learning more about the methods and findings of the Annenberg study can consult the 62-page *Building a Foundation for School Leadership: An Evaluation of the Annenberg Distributed Leadership Project, 2006–2010* (Consortium for Policy Research in Education, August 2012) by Jonathan Supovitz and Matthew Riggan.

Brian A. McNulty and Laura Besser, *Leaders Make It Happen! An Administrator's Guide to Data Teams* (Houghton Mifflin, 2011).

Any distributed leadership structure will rely on data teams to set priorities, measure progress, and make adjustments until a goal is reached. This book shows administrators how to develop data teams and build capacity in faculty through collaborative teamwork to manage and analyze data. Topics discussed include the importance of follow-through, focusing on a limited number of goals and strategies, involving students in the data teams process, and leading the data teams process. Readers will find useful information about using data teams at the district, building, and classroom levels. Each recommended practice is grounded in recent research. Many exhibits and templates support the text.

Tonya C. Balch and Bradley V. Balch, *Building Great School Counselor-Administrator Teams: A Systematic Approach to Supporting Students, Staff, and the Community* (Solution Tree Press, 2019).

In recent years, the roles of school administrators and school counselors have begun to overlap. This book describes how school administrators and counselors can work together as a team to increase their impact on student mental health, student behavior, and school improvement. It is a practical guide that provides a systematic approach to establishing a school administrator–counselor team. Chapters include "Team Effectiveness and Performance," "Ethical Considerations for Different Stakeholders," "Confidentiality," "Abuse and Neglect Reporting and Mitigation," "Crises," and "Parent and Guardian Engagement." Each chapter offers a professional development activity related to the chapter topic.

Afterword

Going Big with the Two-Rules Philosophy

In 2012, I became the director of educational support for our district. In this position, I administered federal grants for the high school, middle schools, and elementary schools. This was a great opportunity for me to expand my two-rules thinking beyond Fall Ridge and support people in many schools. I wanted to take two-rules thinking big in our district.

I approached this job using the two-rules questions. What could I do to make families feel good and feel safe? What could I do to make faculty feel good and feel safe? What could I do to make principals feel good and feel safe? How could I use the grant resources my office administered to give principals and staff the kinds of support we had built at Fall Ridge?

Families

My office added a family liaison position to each of the buildings in the district. These individuals worked with school social workers, guidance counselors, truancy officer, and administrative teams to remove barriers for students. They worked with students and their families on truancy issues; they helped homeless families find resources; they helped families with basic needs such as food, clothing, shelter, and transportation; and they conducted trainings that families and students could attend together about nutrition and recreation. Each liaison received training about how to interact with families. They were instructed to only praise them and to never talk down to anyone or criticize anyone. We wanted the liaisons to create strong relationships with families that would build them up and give them access to many types of resources.

No one had ever made a community calendar for our area that listed free and low-cost opportunities for family activities. I saw that making such a calendar would be a great way to build bridges between the school district and community organizations, businesses, and agencies. For example, we provided free passes to families to a local park which agreed to teach families CPR and water safety protocols. A bowling alley also provided free passes for families. In each of these activities, families were required to attend rather than just the kids or one adult. The idea was to build up families by showing them ways to have quality time together.

We created a Hispanic Day for Hispanic families in our district. One of our family liaisons who was a member of this community organized this day; she had cultural knowledge that ensured that we didn't make a misstep. For example, we held this day at a library in the community instead of in a school to protect the privacy of families who attended. She brought lawyers and paralegals from a nearby city to talk with family members about obtaining citizenship and answer their questions about their specific needs related to that quest. Family members also got information about how to get transportation to the large city in our state where citizenship hearings were held. Nothing was more basic for helping these families feel safe in our community than getting citizenship.

Staff

I changed how we did professional development for staff. Instead of having each principal select what their staff needed, I provided opportunities for staff to choose what kinds of training they got on district-wide professional development day. My staff and I reviewed the data from the needs assessments from all of the schools in the district. (My staff in this position consisted of someone who had been a math teacher, someone who had been a reading teacher, someone who worked with homeless families and English language learners, and a curriculum specialist.) We put all of this information in a spreadsheet so we could see patterns. Then I talked with principals about the needs they were seeing from staff evaluations. After assessing these sources of data, we planned a professional development day that was organized like a conference. Faculty and teaching assistants could choose which sessions they attended instead of sitting through sessions they didn't need or had already had. We had one or two sessions that were mandatory, but for the rest of the day faculty chose which sessions to attend. That year we had a session on how to deal with the effects of poverty in the classroom, another on technology in the classroom, one on math, and one on the needs of special education teachers. We had a session to introduce teaching assistants to scripted interventions they could use in the classroom related to phonemic awareness, phonics, reading comprehension, and math. We had identified that a theme that emerged from all of the schools was difficulty with reading comprehension and writing, so we brought in Kristina Smekens to show teachers how they could address those topics. My district supervisor was very skeptical about this kind of setup, but it was a huge hit with the faculty. For the first time, they felt that their needs had been heard and that the district was giving them respect and some control over their professional development.

Principals

We enhanced the use of data instructional facilitators (DIFs) at each building to support principals and staff. These were teachers who had received excellent ratings on evaluations and whose peers and administrators had high confidence in their abilities. Most were from the core content areas of reading and math. As people were pulled from the teaching staff to become DIFs, the district hired people to replace them in the classroom.

The DIFs kept the progress monitoring the district required on track. They made sure staff had what they needed and were keeping up with lessons and with the schedule. Then they worked on putting data together so the staff could see how students were growing. They helped identify students who needed additional academic support and worked with teachers and Grade-Level Teams to set up interventions to help those students. They worked with Grade-Level Teams to discuss group interventions for students working on the same skill. They also worked with the Building Intervention Team to answer questions about what types of interventions had been tried to support struggling students, whether the families of those students had been invited in to discuss how the school was working to help their child, whether the student was participating in or cooperating with interventions, or any other things the Building Intervention Team needed to know before they made decisions about next steps. In effect, the DIFs were liaisons between teachers and the Building Intervention Team.

DIFs supported principals by coaching individual teachers in specific areas of improvement. This helped with designing intervention plans to support staff. My office worked hard to build capacity at every level.

Another thing we did to support principals was use federal grant money to pay the membership dues to the state principals' association for each principal in the district. That gave them access to networking opportunities with colleagues across the state, professional development trainings, updates about what the state legislature was doing regarding education, and so forth.

Making the Two Rules Your Own

These are just a few ideas about how a two-rules mentality can be expanded to show respect and care for many people in your community and your district. It sounds so simple to approach each situation with thoughts about helping others feel safe and feel good. But those two ideas encompass a lot and can guide you to many ideas and practices. Thinking about using the resources you have in your school to build up students, families, and staff will lead you to new ideas about the role of your school in your community. Forming partnerships with local businesses and agencies to support activities that will help families feel good and feel safe will build bridges that will benefit everyone. Thinking about new sources of support for you in your job may lead you to ideas that your district will be glad to help with.

People are finally realizing that your mental health and the mental health of your teachers and students are precious resources. The aftermath of the Covid pandemic has brought this issue to the fore in the public's mind. We are headed for disaster if principals and teachers leave education in the percentages recent surveys predict. We urgently need ways to help administrators and teachers feel that their work is sustainable, that their talents are valued, and that they have the space they need to do their jobs well. And students urgently need support for their mental health and models of behaviors that will support it. I hope that this book about the easy-to-learn-and-remember two-rules concept will support you as you do the hard but essential work of leading your school and nurturing the people in it.

Appendix A

Building Staff Resilience

Teachers in today's schools live every day with levels of stress that weren't imaginable twenty years ago. Teacher shortages, budget cuts, the possibility of school shootings, pressures from parents after two years of virtual education during the pandemic, increasing difficulty finding work-life balance, and the effects of an increasing poverty rate on students have increased the emotional load teachers carry every day.

Building resilience is as important for staff as it is for students. For each person, the key to developing this skill is knowing what works for them and making time to do those things. The combination of self-awareness and deliberate practice of resilience-building activities are essential for cultivating this skill. You can compare resilience-building activities to exercising: the more you do them, the more resilience you will have to draw from.

The first step in building resilience among your staff is learning self-care to build your own resilience. The open-access edited collection *Cultivating Teacher Resilience* has a good chapter titled "'Head' First: Principal Self-Care to Promote Teacher Resilience" that's available online on the publisher's website at https://link.springer.com/chapter/10.1007/978-981-15-5963-1_12. It lists three areas of focus that will help principals model resilience for staff: training for resilience, managing inner dialogue, and practicing self-care.

Many teachers have been socialized to believe that during times of stress they had to try harder or "power through." This approach is likely to lead to burnout. A collective response to stress that focuses on cultivating resilience skills will lead to a staff that is more interconnected, more focused on positive thinking, and more available emotionally to students.

Examples from *Cultivating Teacher Resilience* describing aspects of teacher resilience are shown in the following table:

Dimension	Examples of Resilience Aspects
Emotional	Not taking things personally Having a sense of humor Ability to bounce back Good emotional regulation
Motivational	Self-belief and confidence Persistence and perseverance Having realistic expectations Being positive and optimistic
Professional	High level of competence and skills Good classroom management skills Ability to facilitate effective learning Being flexible and adaptable
Social	Asking others for assistance Good interpersonal skills Ability to take advice from others Strong professional and personal support networks

Source: Susan Beltman, "Understanding and Examining Teacher Resilience from Multiple Perspectives," in Caroline F. Mansfield, ed., *Cultivating Teacher Resilience: International Approaches, Applications and Impact* (Springer, 2021), 34–35.

This table is a good starting point for thinking about how you can help your staff strengthen their resilience-building skills at work. Here are three examples.

1. *Help staff develop strong networks.* Perhaps your school could develop a local network with another school in your district so that staff members, particularly early-career people, are paired with someone they can rely on for support and ideas when work-related stress levels are high. Often, the experience of being heard and validated can reduce stress and enable a person to pick themselves up and renew their search for solutions.

2. *Foster confidence and self-belief.* Have your teams make a list of their strengths. Write an article in your school newsletter that notes a particular strength of each team. Ask students to write positive things about their team. Then present them on your media platforms on a rotating basis for everyone to see. One year our social worker asked students to record short videos in which they said what they liked about their Grade-Level Team. Our teachers were very surprised and pleased the day I sent them the email that asked them to open that file on their Smartboards. We showed those videos on the large screen in the cafetorium so students could see all the positive things the teams were doing for them. In your communications with parents, tell them about the good work the school's teams are doing with students and how the students are responding. At every opportunity, find ways to publicly acknowledge the work and skill of your teams.

3. *Offer a workshop on building resilience.* In times of stress, people tend to forget the skills they have for strengthening resilience. A workshop that provides a list of resilience-building activities, provides deeper knowledge about resilience, or elicits information from staff about what resilience resources they would like to see at school can provide timely support for the most important resource

your school has—the skilled professionals who provide the safety net for students five days a week.

Here is an idea for an activity that could build resilience within teams.

Team Task Exchange as a Resilience-Building Tool

The team structure lends itself well to practices that cultivate resilience. During times of heavy stress, some tasks can seem almost impossible, even things that are normally easy for a team member to do. Ask your team members to take inventory of the things they do best and the tasks that are challenging. Team members can share these lists and exchange tasks on stressful days. The task list might include communicating with a parent, creating a spreadsheet with contact information for each student's family, selecting a classroom routine for the next day, organizing digital files, writing up notes on the day's observations of students, following up on an intervention the team has made, processing the flow of information from the principal and the district, or writing up a request for professional development.

When a team has an inventory that lists the particular skills and knowledge areas of each member, it becomes clear where opportunities to exchange tasks are. Encourage the team to consider the skills they have based on age and experience. A younger team member who grew up in the digital age may be able to organize a colleague's digital files in folders in just a few minutes. That task might have taken an older colleague twice as long because digital skills aren't second nature to them. In exchange, the more experienced colleague can help an early-career colleague identify why a student is having difficulty with reading comprehension. The experienced colleague has seen this many times and knows which classroom routines work in that situation. The early-career colleague would have needed to spend time reading recent research or perhaps would have tried something that didn't work. This exchange would take 10 or 15 minutes for each colleague to contribute their skills and knowledge and would save each one a great deal of time.

This type of exchange offers numerous resilience-building benefits. First, it relieves a portion of the stress load for team members. Something that is difficult for one team member might be easy for another teammate. But it's important that there be quid pro quo—if a team colleague does something for one member, that member needs to reciprocate. Maybe not that day, but within an agreed-upon time period.

Second, helping others is a great way to build resilience. It reminds the helper person (and in a task exchange, both people are helpers) that they have important contributions to make to the community—in this case, the team family. When someone is feeling stressed and anxious, using their skills to support another person is a great psychological lift. It reminds them of their competence and releases dopamine, a brain chemical that helps alleviate stress, improves mental focus, and supports empathy. (For more on this topic, see Eva Ritvo's article "The Neuroscience of Giving" in *Psychology Today* at https://www.psychologytoday.com/us/blog/vitality/201404/the-neuroscience-giving.)

Third, exchanging tasks keeps the team on track and keeps the data flowing upward to building teams and administrators. This means that even when a team member is overloaded with stress, there won't be delays in interruptions in the multiple levels of attention teams give students.

Finally, a task exchange gives team members practice with asking for help. That skill is very difficult for some people to develop. Practicing it in an environment where team members give help in exchange for getting it is a low-risk way to break down the barriers to requesting help.

Resource List

Elena Aguilar, *Onward: Cultivating Emotional Resilience in Educators* (Jossey-Bass, 2018) and *The Onward Workbook: Daily Activities to Cultivate Your Resilience and Thrive* (Jossey-Bass, 2018).

This is a resilience manual. It covers a broad range of topics related to resilience, including self-knowledge, understanding emotions, building community, mindfulness, self-care, training the brain to focus on the positive, and many more. Aguilar encourages readers to consider resilience at three levels: individual, organizational, and systemic conditions. A companion volume, *The Onward Workbook*, provides over 600 pages of activities and exercises linked to the chapter categories of *Onward*. These two books are valuable resources for resilience builders at every level of skill.

Caroline F. Mansfield, ed., *Cultivating Teacher Resilience: International Approaches, Applications and Impact* (Springer, 2021).

This book is available as a free download on the Google Books platform and for Kindle readers at Amazon.com. The chapter authors draw on a program developed in Australia called BRiTE (Building Resilience in Teacher Education). The chapters are based on evidence from years of research on what works to build teacher resilience. Topics include building resilience in early-career teachers, interventions for developing teacher well-being, and an overview of the training modules the research team developed to help educators build resilience. *Cultivating Teacher Resilience* provides a theoretical, research-based foundation for ways to increase teacher resilience. If you're looking for concrete suggestions, though, you'll want to turn to other sources.

John J. Murphy, *Pulling Together: 10 Rules for High Performance Teamwork* (Sourcebooks, 2010).

Pulling Together is a good resource for teams who want to identify and create an inventory of their strengths. Murphy presents content in short bites for busy educators and asks many questions that will help teams identify what they do best and ways they can improve their skills. It would be a good starting point for a team exchange inventory.

Appendix B

Student and Teacher Workshop Day on Recovering from Trauma

Trauma is a big word. Often we don't know the amount of trauma a student is holding because they haven't found an adult they trust enough to tell their story to. Many students we see every day deserve an Emmy award for concealing their pain. Sometimes they cannot say the words but our hearts can hear what isn't spoken.

The mission of a trauma recovery workshop day is to continue to build levels of trust with students, to discover the keys that will unlock doors to support and resources for students who are living in trauma or who have experienced trauma. The message to students is that tomorrow can be better than today and the future can be brighter because of the work your school will be doing together on trauma recovery workshop day.

Preliminary Planning

Considerations when organizing a student and staff workshop day:

- Based on the total number of students and staff in your building, calculate how many additional people you will need on workshop day to support participants who may need immediate assistance. During a trauma recovery workshop, emotions can be triggered or students may reveal things that will need to be addressed right away (e.g., suicidal ideation, self-harming practices, serious depression, a family issue that requires contact with the Department of Children and Family Services). You will want to have people available to talk with those students right away and make any phone calls to outside agencies that are indicated.

- Given the numbers in your school, how many workshop sessions will you need? The groups should be small enough to make it comfortable for students to ask questions.

- Think about how you will allocate faculty and staff. Do you want students to move through the workshop sessions with members of their Grade-Level Teams? How many faculty should participate in each session?

- Make plans that take into account students in high-needs programs. Make sure you plan the day so students with behavioral needs, learning differences, and disabilities will be able to participate.

Structuring the Day

The structure of the day will be based just like your school schedule for the day. This keeps all of the lunches in order and will take into consideration times for breaks for presenters, staff, and students to take a break.

Consider how you can cover times when students are on a break. Use your additional staff (e.g., principal, assistant principal, dean of students, guidance counselor, social worker, school psychologists, secretaries, school resource office, teaching assistants) to help supervise. If you feel you will need additional support for this workshop day, ask the central office if you can hire floating subs for the day or if the district can send staff to help for this day.

Planning the Structure

Once you have determined how many people are needed to support your workshop day and how many students will be participating, you can begin to design the day and see how it needs to flow. I am a visual, hands-on, talk-it-through creator. I need to use my big whiteboard to draw it out and plug things in so I can move things around to get what I know will work. My administrative leadership always helped me with the foundation, then I would ask my intervention team help with the content of the workshop.

When you are able to do it in this way, you will come out with a great final product. People on your teams will think of things you have not thought of. Examples include the flow of the students during transitions between workshops, bathroom locations for breaks, who will be monitoring for people with immediate needs in each workshop area.

Other considerations during the planning stage:

- How will speakers be checked in to your building?

- When should they report?

- What is your plan B if a speaker doesn't show up or has to cancel at the last minute?

Here's what we did about plan B at Fall Ridge. We decided that it was extremely unlikely that no speakers would show up. Based on that assumption, we created four backup plans. The intervention team worked on creating something for four workshop rooms in the case of speaker absence. They found short video clips on the internet and planned sessions where students and staff could talk about the videos and ask questions. They could also discuss what they were taking away from the workshop so far. Another idea was to buy notebooks so kids could create their own checklists of recovery goals and plans for reaching them.

Selecting Workshop Topics

As you select topics for the workshop, think about what your students, your staff, and your intervention team have been identifying as high needs. Those are the issues the workshop sessions should focus on. Use the two-rules philosophy as your guide: focus on workshops that center on feeling good and feeling safe.

All of our speakers agreed to be videotaped so that staff members who were not able to attend their sessions could see them later. It was also important to record the sessions in case students or staff had questions. The videos were an important record that all of us on staff could refer to if we needed to.

Materials for Workshop Day

Make a journal for each participant. This can be easily generated with a nice cover page that has the title of the workshop and a colorful image. Make a page for each session where students can take notes and jot down ideas (see the following figure) During homeroom in the morning, students and staff can write down questions they may have as they start the day. Then at the end of the day, in a final session, students and staff can ask the speakers questions. As students hear what questions staff are thinking about and staff hear the questions students are thinking about, each group will learn more about how the other group sees the world and the kinds of concerns they have.

Session 1.
Feelings: What are they? How do I know what is good?

Questions I have:

____

____

____

Notes to keep:

____

____

____

Things I would like to share:

____

____

____

One thing I will try:

____

____

____

Sample journal page for workshop day

Consider working with community agencies to source materials to give students. For the session on identifying feelings, is there a short book written for young teens that a community partner would be willing to purchase for each student in your school? A story that would engage them that focuses on feeling would be a good launchpad for follow-up classroom discussions.

Could you work with a local printer to make bookmarks for each student that has a list of resilience skills? Is there a community partner who could provide healthy snacks for the session on self-care?

Sample Workshop Topics

Here is an outline of potential workshop sessions. You will know what topics are best for your school.

Session 1. Feelings: What are they? How do I know what is good?

Identify a local psychologist who can speak about this topic at a level your students will understand. The focus should be on helping your students identify their feelings. Ideally, you will be able to have a discussion with this speaker ahead of time to give them context about the issues that have been coming up at your school. Potential content could include these questions:

- What is anger? What are some ways to handle anger?

- What is anxiety? What are some things students can do when they feel anxious?

- What is guilt? What is the relationship between trauma and guilt? What can a student do to process feeling of guilt after a trauma?

- What does it mean to feel good? What activities can students do to activate the brain chemicals that lead to good feelings?

Session 2. Resilience: How can I build myself up?

Identify a local professional (college professor, doctor, educator, judge) who can speak to students about ways to work each day on building up strength to overcome adversity. I used a judge because I knew his story. I knew he would not mind sharing with staff and students about how he built his resilience. A local individual who has overcome some hardships the kids can identify with is a great resource to help them see that it can be done and to see that building up resilience is something they can start working on right away.

Session 3. Self-Care: There is only one you!

Connect with the local health department or an extension office. (I did both.) This session could consist of brief talks about nutrition for your body and mind. It should familiarize students with the relationship between good nutrition and a healthy body and a healthy mind and that this is particularly important when we are under stress. The people who spoke at this session of our workshop day added exercise and talked about techniques students could use at school to help calm themselves, such as breathing exercises, counting, thinking of things that spark happiness, fidgets, and calming music. The speakers for this session gave us quite a few good ideas of things we could provide in classrooms to support students who were working to gain control of their emotions.

We also had an individual on staff who was a trained yoga instructor. We scheduled a break in the gym right after this session where students met up with the physical education staff for yoga training.

Session 4. Structured Activity

After learning about new information all day, students (and staff) will welcome something lighter, a hands-on activity that students and staff can do together. They will need an outlet, a fun activity that generates feel-good brain chemicals and at the same time builds trust. Here are two ideas.

Buddy Walk

Divide the group into pairs and designate one teammate as the walker. Set up an obstacle course. You can use things like tables, chairs, toys, cones, or anything else you have on hand.

Without stepping on or bumping into anything or anyone, the walker must move backward through the course. This is only possible with the help of the partner. The walkers must trust that their partner will guide them safely throughout the course. If a walker turns around while on the course, steps on something, or bumps into anything, the pair has to start over. When a team makes it through the obstacle course successfully, they can switch places and navigate the course again.

This activity becomes age-appropriate for younger children if you create an area that requires walking forward to step over, climb under, move around, and go through obstacles. Have the walker close their eyes, or use blindfolds, so that the buddy can guide them through the course.

This activity could be modified so a small group of students is guiding a faculty member through the course.

Source: "Ten Trust-Building Exercises for Kids and Teens," Healthline, https://www.healthline.com/health/parenting/trust-exercices-for-kids#trust-fall

Team Pen

Team Pen is a perfect in-classroom team building activity.

The teacher will need to tape strings to a large pen before the activity begins.

Students will be placed into teams and each student will hold on to one of the strings connected to the pen.

The teacher will give each group a word to write on a piece of blank paper.

The students within the group will have to navigate the pen together to write the word.

Start out with easy and short words at first but eventually once the kids get better at it this can be a great way to help students practice for their spelling tests or phonics work.

The best part of this activity is seeing what the word ends up looking like once the students are done. This is such a fun activity I can hear the laughter from here!

You can see a video of a group of students doing Team Pen and hear the guiding words from their teacher on the Best-KidsSolutions website.

Source: "16 Team Building Activities For Middle School (With Video Examples)," BestKidsSolutions.com, https://www.bestkidssolutions.com/team-building-activities-for-middle-school/.

End of the Day

Whether your school is large or small, it is a good idea to bring everyone together for the final period of the day. Students have been hearing new ideas in small groups all day, and bringing everyone together reminds them that everyone at their school, including their teachers, is working on the same issues. It is good to end the day with a message of hope that everyone hears together.

Here is what I told students at Fall Ridge:

> As you arrive in your homerooms tomorrow, you will receive a mirror that you can place in your locker. It is magnetic. Here is what I would like for you to know for today:
>
> What you see in the mirror is someone I am proud of every day. You come to our school to work as a member of our school family. You are part of the solution and you work hard each day to make the best choices for yourself and others so everyone will feel good and feel safe.
>
> I want you to reflect on all of the things you learned today. Practice something you learned today. Say to yourself when you look in the mirror, "Today is a great day because I am here."
>
> Look in the mirror and see the reflection we see. Smile. Turn off all of the negative thoughts and words you hear. Let my words replace any negative messages you hear: "I will never give up on you. I believe in you."
>
> Today you have begun learning how to heal from trauma. You have learned skills and have heard about ways to support well-being and self-care so you can be the best you can be. There is only one you! You are an important member of our school family. All of us need to work to keep ourselves as healthy as possible. We want to eat right, exercise, get plenty of rest, and nurture ourselves.

I know that during your sessions all of you were asking questions. I hope you realized today that we are all working together on many of the same things so we can be healthy. We all have stories. That is what life is all about. Each of the adults you know in this building was a child at one time who had struggles as they grew into adulthood.

We have so much more to talk about, so our conversations will not end here today. In fact, I think they are just beginning. Please take some time to think about today. Write down any questions you have and your teachers can get them to me so we can ask the speakers from today to answer them. Your teachers may also be able to answer some of your questions.

When it is close to dismissal time, release the lowest grade level first. Allow them time to get out of the gym or auditorium with staff so they can retrieve items from lockers and then exit to buses or cars or their walking route. You can continue to speak to the remaining students during this time. Then repeat with the next grade level in the same way.

After the Workshop

The next day, when students are in their homerooms, they can complete a survey about the day. Have both staff and students complete it. In the survey, provide an opportunity for suggestions of additional topics to cover and other ideas to support all of the students and staff, taking into account cultures, genders, education needs, and other factors.

The survey can gather data about which sessions students liked and why they liked them. You could also gather data about what concepts students learned in each session so you can gauge whether the speakers delivered their messages effectively. The survey can also ask for students' suggestions about how to make this workshop day better in the future.

Provide students with an opportunity to work together on a project about their experiences from workshop day. Let students brainstorm together about ideas for how they can share what they learned in the workshop with others.

Ideas for possible extensions after the workshop:

- Compose letters to legislators asking for more support for mental health in all schools and incentives for people to go into mental health professions to work in schools

- Create a video to help other teens with what they have learned

- Design posters to display in the school and in other areas within the community

- Write poems or short stories

- Make graphic design cartoons

Appendix C

List of Programs Approved by the National Association of School Psychologists

Given the current shortage of school psychologists, principals need to think outside the box to provide supports for student mental health. One way is to form a partnership with a nearby university to provide in-person or virtual training for staff, organize virtual support for students, or line up internships with degree-granting programs. This list from the website of the National Association of School Psychologists provides the names of institutions that offer programs or advanced degrees in school psychology. The page (https://www.nasponline.org/standards-and-certification/graduate-program-approval-and-accreditation/program-approval/approved-programs) provides links to each school, department, or program.

The NASP website provides other resources about the roles school psychologists can play in school-community partnerships:

- Blog post by a school psychologist: "Beyond the Classroom and into the Community" (https://www.nasponline.org/research-and-policy/policy-matters-blog/beyond-the-classroom-and-into-the-community)

- PDF titled "Nine Elements of Effective School Community Partnerships to Address Student Mental Health, Physical Health, and Overall Wellness" (available from the NASP website)

- PDF titled "Effective School-Community Partnerships to Support School Mental Health" (available from the NASP website)

These resources may give you ideas about how to structure a school-community partnership for student mental health that will work for your school.

Alabama

University of Alabama, Tuscaloosa

Arizona

Northern Arizona University, Flagstaff
University of Arizona, Tucson

Arkansas

University of Central Arkansas, Conway

California

Azusa Pacific University, Murrieta
California State University–Chico
California State University–Long Beach
California State University–Los Angeles
California State University–North Ridge
California State University–Sacramento
Loyola Marymount University, Los Angeles

San Diego University
University of California, Berkeley
University of California–Riverside
University of California–Santa Barbara

Colorado

University of Colorado, Denver
University of Denver
University of Northern Colorado, Greeley

Connecticut

Fairfield University
Southern Connecticut State University, Hartford
University of Connecticut, Storrs
University of Hartford

Delaware

University of Delaware, Newark
District of Columbia
Gallaudet University

Florida

Barry University, Miami Shores
Florida International University, Miami
Nova Southeastern University, Fort Lauderdale
University of Central Florida, Orlando
University of Florida, Gainesville
University of South Florida, Tampa

Georgia

Georgia Southern University, Statesboro
Georgia State University, Atlanta
University of Georgia, Athens

Idaho

Idaho State University, Pocatello

Illinois

Eastern Illinois University, Charleston
Illinois State University, Normal
Loyola University–Chicago
Northern Illinois University, DeKalb
Southern Illinois University–Edwardsville

Indiana

Ball State University, Muncie
Indiana State University, Terre Haute
Indiana University–Bloomington
Valparaiso University

Iowa

University of Iowa, Iowa City
University of Northern Iowa, Cedar Falls

Kansas

University of Kansas, Lawrence
Wichita State University

Kentucky

Murray State University
University of Kentucky, Lexington
Western Kentucky University, Bowling Green

Louisiana

Louisiana State University, Baton Rouge
Louisiana State University–Shreveport
Nicholls State University, Thibodeaux

Maryland

Bowie State University
Towson University
University of Maryland–College Park

Massachusetts

William James College, Newton

Northeastern University, Boston

Tufts University, Medford

University of Massachusetts–Amherst

Worcester State University

Michigan

Andrews University, Berrien Springs

Central Michigan University, Mount Pleasant

Grand Valley State University, Allendale

Michigan State University, East Lansing

Wayne State University, Detroit

Minnesota

Minnesota State University–Mankato

Minnesota State University–Moorhead

University of Minnesota, Minneapolis

Mississippi

Mississippi State University

University of Southern Mississippi, Hattiesburg

Missouri

University of Missouri–Columbia

Montana

University of Montana, Missoula

Nebraska

University of Nebraska–Kearney

University of Nebraska–Lincoln

University of Nebraska–Omaha

Nevada

University of Nevada–Las Vegas

New Hampshire

Plymouth State University

New Jersey

Fairleigh Dickinson University, Teaneck

Georgian Court University, Lakewood

Kean University, Union

Montclair State University

New Jersey City University, Jersey City

Rider University, Lawrenceville

Rowan University, Glassboro

Rutgers University

New Mexico

New Mexico State University

New York

Adelphi University, Garden City

Brooklyn College

Columbia University, Teachers College, New York

Fordham University–Lincoln Center, Manhattan

Hofstra University, Hampstead

Iona College, New Rochelle and Bronxville

Marist College, Poughkeepsie

Mercy College, Dobbs Ferry

Niagara University

Pace University, New York

Queens College–CUNY

Roberts Wesleyan College, Rochester

State University of New York–Oswego

Syracuse University

Yeshiva University, New York

North Carolina

Appalachian State University, Boone

East Carolina University, Greeneville

North Carolina State University, Raleigh

University of North Carolina–Chapel Hill

Western Carolina University, Cullowhee

North Dakota

Minot State University

Ohio

Cleveland State University

John Carroll University, University Heights

Kent State University

Miami University

Ohio State University, Columbus

University of Cincinnati

University of Dayton

University of Toledo

Youngstown University

Oklahoma

Oklahoma State University, Stillwater

Southwestern Oklahoma State University, Weatherford

University of Central Oklahoma, Edmond

Oregon

Lewis & Clark College, Portland

University of Oregon, Eugene

Pennsylvania

Duquesne University, Pittsburgh

Indiana University of Pennsylvania

Lehigh University, Bethlehem
Millersville University of Pennsylvania
Pennsylvania State University, State College
PennWest California
PennWest Edinboro
Philadelphia College of Osteopathic Medicine
Temple University, Philadelphia

South Carolina
The Citadel, Charleston
Francis Marion University, Florence
University of South Carolina, Columbia
Winthrop University, Rock Hill

South Dakota
University of South Dakota, Vermillion

Tennessee
Middle Tennessee State University, Murfreesboro
University of Memphis
University of Tennessee–Chattanooga
University of Tennessee–Knoxville

Texas
Abilene Christian University
Sam Houston State University, Huntsville
Stephen F. Austin State University, Nacogdoches
Texas A&M University, College Station
Texas State University–San Marco
Texas Woman's University, Denton
Trinity University, San Antonio
University of Houston–Clear Lake
University of Texas–Austin

Utah
Brigham Young University, Provo
University of Utah, Salt Lake City
Utah State University, Logan

Virginia
College of William and Mary, Williamsburg
George Mason University, Fairfax
James Madison University, Harrisonburg
Radford University
University of Virginia, Charlottesville

Washington
Central Washington University, Ellensburg
Seattle University
University of Washington, Seattle

West Virginia
Marshall University, Huntington

Wisconsin
University of Wisconsin–Eau Clare
University of Wisconsin–Madison
University of Wisconsin–Stout

Appendix D

Coping with Feelings When You Can't Help a Student

Sometimes your best efforts and your love for a student aren't enough to help them. They have sustained too much damage before you met them or they have a genetic mental illness that will take them out of your school. It's difficult to process the complex feelings you probably have after pouring everything you have into a child and then watching them go to jail or a full-time residential care facility at such a young age.

Logan Miller and Logan Wright were two boys in the same grade. They lived in the same neighborhood and had very similar lifestyles at home. Their families were the same socioeconomic status, they were both white, they lived in the same neighborhood, and their parents had similarly low levels of education. Their fathers had both dropped out of high school. Both boys were receiving special education support.

Logan M. was a small-framed boy with strawberry blond hair and freckles. He was the oldest of four children. He was being raised by his father with some support from grandparents. He was a simple child and did not have a lot. He wanted to be the protector of his siblings and always tried to stand up for them.

Logan W. was a large-framed boy with dark blond hair and freckles. He had older siblings, but mostly he spent time with his younger brother, who was home with him all of the time. He was being raised by a mother and father. His father was a truck driver who was away from home a great deal. A grandmother would step in to help at times. Logan W. was loud and worked to be funny. He liked to have attention. He often would do something and find himself in trouble, then he would pour on the charm to say he did not mean it, that he was sorry and would not do it again.

Both Logans caught the bus at the same bus stop each day. Logan W.'s grandmother was a bus driver for the school district and this gave him a feeling of power. He thought this gave him an advantage and believed he could do what he wanted to do. That is where his bullying began.

At the bus stop each morning, Logan W. began to say things to Logan M. "You are so little." "Why don't you have a mom?" "Why don't you have different clothes or shoes to wear? You wear the same things every day."

Logan M. arrived at school each day very angry. He did not want to interact with anyone in the class and the classroom teacher was having a difficult time communicating with him. One day he was sent to the office. I found him sitting in the office chair waiting to talk to the dean of students.

"Good morning, Logan. I am happy to see you today, but what brings you to the office?"

"I am mad today. I think I am mad a lot of the days."

"I see. May I ask what is making you mad?"

"I don't want to talk about it."

"Okay, I understand. I don't always like to talk about things that make me mad either. It takes me a little time to work through my emotions." I paused for a long moment to give Logan some time to calm down.

"Logan, would you like to have a drink and a little snack? I have some over in the cabinet if you want to pick something out."

Logan chose a drink and a snack and began to eat and drink.

"Logan, let me know when you are ready to talk to me. I will listen and give you all my attention."

After a few minutes he began to speak.

"Mrs. Yoho, you know where I live, don't you?"

"Yes, I do. Over in Cremont."

"Yeah. Do you know all of the other kids who live over there by me?

"Well, I think I do. You are testing my memory today! Are you trying to see how much I know? Is this a trivia game?"

Logan chuckled. "You make me laugh sometimes. Well, I am mad because of one of the kids in my neighborhood who catches the bus with us every day, he is just mean." He tightened his fists and his face got red.

"I am sorry, Logan. You can always tell us about things like that. This is a problem and we can work to find a solution to this situation."

"I am afraid that would just make it worse. He doesn't do anything here at school, only when we are at the bus stop."

"What does he do at the bus stop?"

"He says stuff to me, he makes fun of me, and it just keeps getting to be more and more. I know my face gets red and I clench my fists and I get to the point where I want to hit him. He is bigger than I am, but I can't take much more."

"Oh, Logan, I am so sorry. Let's have you talk with Ms. J. [the school social worker] today. Then we can work on a solution for you. I am going to talk with Logan W. I will not say I have spoken to you, I just want to see what he tells me about himself."

Later, I called Logan W. to the office to ask him how things were going for him.

"Hi, Logan, how are you today?"

"I am good, Mrs. Yoho. Am I in trouble?"

"No, why? Did you do something you think you should be in trouble for and need to talk to me?"

"I don't think so."

"It is always good to think and reflect to make sure. You always want to make sure you are saying and doing things to make others feel good and feel safe." Logan moved in his chair and we had an uncomfortable wait time.

"I can't think of anything here at school."

"Can you think of anything at any other place you go? I noticed you said here at school."

I waited some more. He moved in his seat and his face began to get red.

"Well, maybe."

"Okay, what would that be?"

"Well, I may say some teasing things to one of the kids in our neighborhood at the bus stop, but I am just joking around."

"I see, so he is laughing with you when you are saying these things?"

"Well, I don't see him laugh, but he doesn't say anything."

"Does he know you are joking?"

"I don't know."

"Well, maybe we should talk about it."

"Yeah, I think we can."

I called Ms. J. and asked if she and Logan M. could join Logan W. and me in my office.

We all gathered around the table to discuss the situation.

"Boys, I brought you together because one of the teachers noticed a change in the behavior of one of you. All of us pay attention to everything about you. We care not only about your learning, but also about your well-being. So we want you to feel good and feel safe everywhere you go."

Ms. J. said, "I would like to take time to work with both of you boys throughout the school year individually. I believe you have some things in common and could help each other. It would be great to talk about this at some lunches together and we can ask Mrs. M. [the school psychologist] to help us out at lunch time."

"That sounds like a great long-term plan, Ms. J. I would like for you two to talk to each other about what is going on at the bus stop. What

I think is the best way to approach a situation when someone is doing something that is not making you feel good or feel safe is this. Use *I* sentences. Like this: 'I do not feel good when you say . . .' or 'I do not feel safe when you . . .' *I* messages are great because they help you put into words exactly what you are trying to say."

The boys began talking with each other using *I* messages. After that, the boys calmed down and things improved with them for a short time. However, Logan W. and his younger brother Brody both were having difficulties socializing with others. They started acting out more and more. One day Brody took a pair of scissors into his classroom and began cutting on his arm. We dismissed the students from the room and called for an ambulance and for help from the police. Another day Brody brought a pellet gun to the bus stop and was shooting it at some of the girls.

Both boys were hospitalized for mental health evaluations. Professionals determined that Logan W. was homicidal and that Brody, who was in the sixth grade, was bipolar and had borderline psychotic tendencies. They were both placed in institutions and the family left the area. After Logan was placed, we had a conference call with Logan's doctor at his mental hospital to discuss his case. The director of special education, Logan's special education teacher, the school social worker, the school psychologist, Logan's mother, and I all participated on this call. The doctor wanted to know who in our meeting Mrs. Yoho was. I said, "I am here." The doctor stated, "Well, I just wanted to let you know he absolutely loves you and talks about you all of the time. Based on my experiences with individuals with this level of mental illness, I will say that if he is released from here and returns to the school, the person who he will seek to harm will be you. These individuals usually kill the people they love the most."

Logan M. continued to grow stronger after his bullying experience and learned how to talk through the issues he faced. He continued to see Ms. J. as he went through middle school. He developed strategies to help him learn to set both short, achievable goals and long-term goals; use positive self-talk; use two-rules questions when facing problems;

identify what he was feeling and what those emotions meant; use strategies for calming down; and express himself through art, music, and exercise (he loved basketball). These new skills supported Logan M. as he moved from middle school to high school.

This was a hard situation where we were able to help one student but not two others. I felt grief about Logan and Brody W. They were so young to be ill enough to be removed from society and their diagnoses were so hard to hear. On the one hand, the systems in place at Fall Ridge had helped flag these brothers' behavior and the outcome was that they didn't harm any students or adults seriously. On the other hand, they both had a long road ahead of them to find a peaceful life that might contain moments of joy and happiness.

This is a topic you won't see too much about in the literature for principals. We love our students and want to help them. We want our schools to be places that prepare them for adulthood. We want to feel that we play a part in helping children become people who contribute to their community. When it becomes clear that that won't be the outcome for a student, at least not right away, we may feel that we failed, that we could have done more. And we may feel tremendous sadness for the student and even for ourselves. We want to succeed! It's hard to accept that our best efforts aren't enough for some students.

In situations like the one with Logan and Brody W., I would remind myself of a concept I frequently discussed with Fall Ridge teachers: the power of our words. When you are absolutely authentic with a student and that student knows in their bones that you care deeply for them, your words have tremendous power. Those children carry your encouragement and support and belief in them as they move through life, even—perhaps especially—when their path takes them to hard places. More than once I have heard from caregivers or medical providers for a child who was in juvenile detention or a mental hospital that they talked about me all the time, that they loved me and cherished our time together. Our words can be a light that children carry into dark places.

Our efforts will not always yield the results we are looking for, and that is a hard truth to accept. But it is also true that we will never know the impact our efforts will have on the rest of the lives of our students, especially those who walk hard paths at an early age. The love and support you pour into a child is never wasted. It stays with them for the rest of their lives.

Another thing I would remind myself is that I was never the savior of a child. I and my staff worked to give each student the best we had to offer, but we didn't "lose" children or "save" them. The resources we poured into our students were theirs to do with as they chose. They were gifts with no strings attached. The choice of what to do with those resources always belonged fully with each child. We were just helpers along the way. Our role was to guide, not direct.

I thank you for reading these pages, for learning all you can to support those you serve and being the solution for so many who need you. If not you, then who will help children figure out where to go from here? The issues have only grown bigger and wider since the days I was in the trenches. I am here to support you in the work you do that saves lives every day. You can never know how many students see their positive, warm interactions with you as a lifeline that is helping them survive their daily traumas and struggles. And you will never know how often that love and support carries a child—and later, an adult—through a hard and heavy time.

In a school with countless rules, troubles arose,
Frustrated teachers, angry children, and woes,
Unseen, unnoticed, the trauma, the pain,
Burdened hearts in a cycle of strain.
Principals, too, felt the weight of the demands,
Aching hearts seeking ways to lend helping hands,
Amidst the chaos, a question arose,
Could there be a remedy to heal and compose?
Two rules, they proposed, for hearts to embrace,
To bring solace and harmony in this crowded space,
A rule to feel good, to uplift and inspire,
A rule to feel safe, quelling fear's raging fire.
Questions became the key, the catalyst for change,
Pause and reflect, before actions estrange,
How will this make me, or others, feel?
A crucial choice, to wound or to heal.
The power lies within, the choices we make,
To be part of solutions, or problems to take,
The path is clear, though challenges may loom,
Choose wisely, and illuminate the room.
Let empathy guide us, and kindness prevail,
A simple shift in perspective can unveil,
The impact we hold in our words and our deeds,
A ripple of goodness, fulfilling our needs.
For in this world, where rules may abound,
Let compassion and understanding resound,
Together, united, we can make a stand,
To foster a haven, with love at hand.
So let us abide by these rules so wise,
To feel good and safe, a heartfelt prize,
With questions as beacons, guiding our way,
We'll transform darkness into a brighter day.

Endnotes

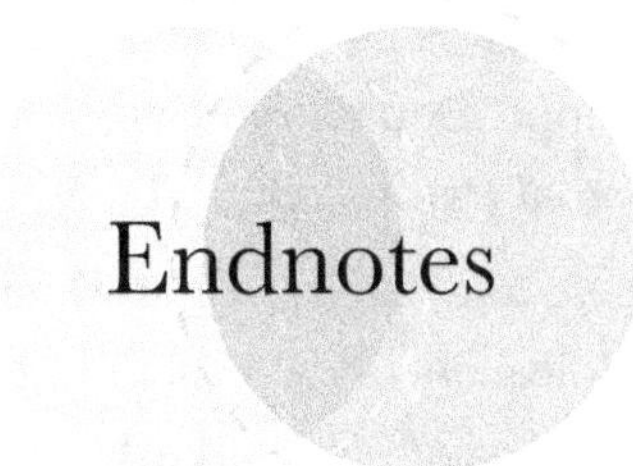

Introduction

[1]This is a pseudonym.

[2]"The Impact of Active Shooter Drills in Schools: Time to Rethink Reactive School Safety Strategies," Everytown Research & Policy, September 3, 2020, last updated February 20, 2023, bit.ly/3VC93st.

[3]"The Impact of Active Shooter Drills in Schools."

[4]David P. Hurford, Rick Lindskog, AmyKay Cole, Robyn Jackson, Sara Thomasson, and Amanda Wade, "The Role of School Climate in School Violence: A Validity Study of a Web-Based School Violence Survey," *Journal of Educational Research & Policy Studies* 10, no. 1 (2010): 51–77.

Chapter 2

[1]Jaana Juvonen, Vi-Nhuan Le, Tessa Kaganoff, Catherine Augustine and Louay Constant, *Focus on the Wonder Years: Challenges Facing the American Middle School* (Santa Monica, CA: RAND Corporation, 2004), 47.

[2]D. Cole, "Relation of Social and Academic Competence to Depressive Symptoms in Childhood," *Journal of Abnormal Psychology* 99 (1990): 422–429;

S. Nolen-Hoksema, M. E. P. Seligman, and J. S. Girgus, "Predictors and Consequences of Childhood Depressive Symptoms: A 5-Year Longitudinal Study," *Journal of Abnormal Psychology* 101 (1992): 405–422.

[3]R. W. Roeser, J. S. Eccles, and C. Freedman-Doan, "Academic Functioning and Mental Health in Adolescence: Patterns, Progressions, and Routes from Childhood," *Journal of Adolescent Research* 14 (1999): 135–174.

[4]K. Aunola, H. Stattin, and J. E. Nurmi, "Adolescents' Achievement Strategies, School Adjustment, and Externalizing and Internalizing Problem Behaviors," *Journal of Youth and Adolescence* 29 (2000): 289–306; M. H. Shann, "Academics and a Culture of Caring: The Relationship between School Achievement and Prosocial and Antisocial Behaviors in Four Urban Middle Schools," *School Effectiveness and School Improvement* 10 (1999): 390–413.

[5]R. Haskins, T. Walden, and C. T. Ramey, "Teacher and Student Behavior in High- and Low-Ability Groups," *Journal of Educational Psychology* 75 (1983): 865–867; T. Kershaw, "The Effects of Educational Tracking on the Social Mobility of African Americans," *Journal of Black Studies* 23 (1992): 125–169.

[6]B. D. Cairns, and R. D. Cairns, *Lifelines and Risks: Pathways of Youth in Our Time* (New York: Cambridge University Press, 1994); J. G. Dryfoos, *Adolescents at Risk: Prevalence and Prevention* (New York: Oxford University Press, 1990); M. Roderick, *The Path to Dropping Out: Evidence for Intervention* (Westport, Conn.: Auburn House, 1993).

[7]"Eva's Definition of Forgiveness," CANDLES Holocaust Museum and Education Center, https://candlesholocaustmuseum.org/our-survivors/eva-kor/forgiveness/.

Chapter 3

[1]Chapter 6 discusses intervention teams in detail.

[2]You can see Michael McMillan's short video about the pink-bat approach to solving problems on YouTube at https://www.youtube.com/watch?v=X-epR6sNHkio&feature=emb_logo.

Chapter 4

[1]"Children and Youth in the United States Are Frequently Exposed to Traumatic Experiences," May 16, 2018, Substance Abuse and Mental Health Services Administration, https://www.samhsa.gov/sites/default/files/brief_report_natl_childrens_mh_awareness_day.pdf.

[2]Vincent J. Felitti, Robert F. Anda, MD, Dale Nordenberg, David F. Williamson, Alison M. Spitz, Valerie Edwards, Mary P. Koss, and James S. Marks, "Relationship of Childhood Abuse and Household Dysfunction to Many of the Leading Causes of Death in Adults: The Adverse Childhood Experiences (ACE) Study," *American Journal of Preventive Medicine* 14, no. 4 (1988): 1609–1613. The authors were associated with the Department of Preventive Medicine, Southern California Permanente Medical Group (Kaiser Permanente), the National Center for Chronic Disease Prevention and Health Promotion at the Centers for Disease Control and Prevention, the Department of Pediatrics at the Emory University School of Medicine, and the Department of Family and Community Medicine at the University of Arizona Health Sciences Center.

[3]These factors were "smoking, severe obesity, physical inactivity, depressed mood, and suicide attempts." Felitti et al., "Relationship of Childhood Abuse and Household Dysfunction to Many of the Leading Causes of Death in Adults," 249.

[4]Felitti et al., "Relationship of Childhood Abuse and Household Dysfunction to Many of the Leading Causes of Death in Adults," 251.

[5]Dimitra Hartas, "Critically Revisiting the Foundational Studies on Adverse Childhood Experiences," The Social Policy Blog, October 7, 2019, https://socialpolicyblog.com/2019/10/07/critically-revisiting-the-foundational-studies-on-adverse-childhood-experiences/. Hartas's blog post is based on an article with the same title in *Social Policy and Society* 18, no. 3 (2019).

[6]Hartas, "Critically Revisiting the Foundational Studies on Adverse Childhood Experiences."

[7]Felitti et al., "Relationship of Childhood Abuse and Household Dysfunction to Many of the Leading Causes of Death in Adults," 255.

[8]Kathryn Ashton, Alisha R. Davies, Karen Hughes, Kat Ford, Andrew Cotter-Roberts, and Mark A. Bellis, "Adult Support during Childhood: A Retrospective Study of Trusted Adult Relationships, Sources of Personal Adult Support and Their Association with Childhood Resilience Resources," *BMC Psychology* 9 (2021): article 101, https://bmcpsychology.biomedcentral.com/articles/10.1186/s40359-021-00601-x#MOESM1.

[9]Brooklyn Raney, *One Trusted Adult: How to Build Strong Connections & Healthy Boundaries with Young People* (Circle Talk Publishing, 2019).

[10]The Department of Justice defines community policing as a practice that "promotes organizational strategies that support the systematic use of partnerships and problem-solving techniques to proactively address the immediate conditions that give rise to public safety issues such as crime, social disorder, and fear of crime." Law enforcement employees who practice community policing work to establish collaborative partnerships with community members in order to solve problems before they escalate into crime. U.S. Department of Justice, "Community Policing Defined," /https://cops.usdoj.gov/RIC/Publications/cops-p157-pub.pdf.

[11]"Rita Pierson Relationships," YouTube video, https://www.youtube.com/watch?v=fU2gRR7MBIw.

Chapter 5

[1]Kathleen Phillips, Julie Dietz, Mark Brown, and Gaye Harrison, "I Sing the Body Electric: Description of an Innovative Health Promotion and Fine Arts Program for Adolescents," *International Electronic Journal of Health Education* 9 (2006): 157.

[2]Phillips et al., "I Sing the Body Electric," 162.

[3]Susan E. Craig, *Trauma-Sensitive Schools: Learning Communities Transforming Children's Lives, K–5* (New York: Teachers College Press, 2016), 89.

[4]The information in this paragraph comes from Education Commission of the States, "State K–3 Policies: What Are the Mental Health and Trauma Training Requirements for K-3 Teachers?" https://files.eric.ed.gov/fulltext/ED608357.pdf.

[5]Richard Morin, "America's Middle-Class Meltdown," *Washington Post*, December 1, 1991, https://www.washingtonpost.com/archive/opinions/1991/12/01/americas-middle-class-meltdown/5ed5f8b6-d9ac-4282-b3d8-166cf-2c1e80a/.

[6]Morin, "America's Middle-Class Meltdown."

[7]"3.4 Million More Children in Poverty in February 2022 than December 2021," Center on Poverty and Social Policy at Columbia University, March 23, 2022, https://www.povertycenter.columbia.edu/news-internal/monthly-poverty-february-2022#:~:text=Monthly%20poverty%20remained%20elevated%20in,poverty%20rate%20of%2012.5%20percent.

[8]Susan Perkins and Sandra Graham-Bermann, "Violence Exposure and the Development of School-Related Functioning: Mental Health, Neurocognition, and Learning," *Aggression and Violent Behavior* 17, no. 1 (2012): 81–98.

Chapter 6

[1]In 2005, Michael S. Repie quoted a 1999 study that estimated that "10 percent of children in the general education population may have a psychiatric disorder." Repie, "A School Mental Health Issues Survey from the Perspective of Regular and Special Education Teachers, School Counselors, and School Psychologists," *Education and Treatment of Children* 28, no. 3 (2005): 279–298, quote on 279. In the same special issue of *Education and Treatment of Children*, Carrie Masia-Warner, Douglas W. Nangle, and David J. Hansen reported that "approximately 21%" of children aged 9 to 17 had "diagnosable psychiatric disorders." "Bringing Evidence-Based Child Mental Health Services to the Schools: General Issues and Specific Populations," *Education and Treatment of Children* 28, no. 3 (2005): 165–172, quote on 172.

[2]Howard S. Edelman and Linda Taylor, "Toward a Comprehensive Policy Vision for Mental Health in Schools," in *Handbook of School Mental Health: Advancing Practice and Research*, edited by Mark D. Weist, Steven W. Evans, and Nancy Lever (Springer, 2000), 30.

[3]Email from a Fall Ridge teacher, February 23, 2023.

⁴R. Marc A. Crundwell and Kim Killu, "Responding to a Student's Depression," ACSD 68, no. 2 (2010), https://www.ascd.org/el/articles/responding-to-a-students-depression.

⁵Aliza Werner-Seidler, Yael Perry, Alison L. Calear, Jill M. Newby, and Helen Christensen, "School-Based Depression and Anxiety Prevention Programs for Young People: A Systematic Review and Meta-Analysis," *Clinical Psychology Review* 51 (February 2017): 30–47, https://www.sciencedirect.com/science/article/pii/S0272735815301409.

⁶"Teen Suicide," America's Health Rankings, https://www.americashealthrankings.org/explore/health-of-women-and-children/measure/teen_suicide. See also Gil Zalsman, Keith Hawton, Danuta Wassterman, Kees van Heeringen, Ella Arensman, and Marco Sarciapone, "Suicide Prevention Strategies Revisited: 10-Year Systematic Review," *The Lancet* 3, no. 7 (2016): P646–659.

⁷Michael Rothfield and Christina Caron, "After Teen's Suicide, A New Jersey Community Grapples with Bullying," *New York Times*, February 13, 2023, https://www.nytimes.com/2023/02/13/nyregion/nj-teen-suicide-bullying-school.html.

⁸Deitra Reiser, Katherine Cowan, Stacy Skalski, and Mary Beth Klotz, "A More Valuable Resource," *Principal Leadership* (November 2010): 12–16.

⁹U.S. Bureau of Labor Statistics, "Occupational Employment and Wages, May 2021: 19-3034 School Psychologists," https://www.bls.gov/oes/curren/oes193034.htm; National Center for Education Statistics, "Fast Facts: Educational Institutions," https://nces.ed.gov/fastfacts/display.asp?id=84.

¹⁰D. E. Boccio, G. Weisz, and R. Lefkowitz, "Administrative Pressure to Practice Unethically and Burnout within the Profession of School Psychology," *Psychology in the Schools* 53 (2016): 659–672. For more about the challenges of retaining school psychologists, see NASP: "Shortages in School Psychology: Challenges to Meeting the Growing Needs of U.S. Students and Schools" (link available at https://apps.nasponline.org/search-results.aspx?q=Shortages+in+School+Psychology).

Chapter 7

[1] Michael Hobbs, "The Importance of Principals: Review Identifies Practices, Behavior of Effective School Leaders," UNC School of Education, August 31, 2022, https://ed.unc.edu/2022/08/31/edge-the-importance-of-principals/.

[2] "Prioritizing Instructional Leadership," The Principal's Playbook, n.d., https://www.theprincipalsplaybook.com/instructional-leadership/prioritizing-instructional-leadership-as-a-principal.

[3] John Corrigan and Mark Merry, "Principal Leadership in a Time of Change," *Frontiers in Education*, May 11, 2022, https://www.frontiersin.org/articles/10.3389/feduc.2022.897620/full.

[4] Zachary Scott Robins, "How School Leaders Can Navigate Conflicting Demands This Year," Edutopia, October 15, 2021, https://www.edutopia.org/article/how-school-leaders-can-navigate-conflicting-demands-year/.

[5] "Building a Culture of Success: What Effective Principals Do," Florida Tax Watch, September 1, 2022, https://floridataxwatch.org/Research/Full-Library/ArtMID/34407/ArticleID/19200/Building-a-Culture-of-Success-What-Effective-Principals-Do.

[6] "NASSP's Survey of America's School Leaders and High School Students."

[7] Emily Tate Sullivan, "Principals Are on the Brink of a Breakdown," EdSurge, July 6, 2022, https://www.edsurge.com/news/2022-07-06-principals-are-on-the-brink-of-a-breakdown#:~:text=A%20recent%20survey%20found%2085,percent%20are%20dealing%20with%20burnout.

[8] "NASSP's Survey of America's School Leaders and High School Students."

[9] Sullivan, "Principals Are on the Brink of a Breakdown."

[10] Sullivan, "Principals Are on the Brink of a Breakdown."

[11] "NASSP's Survey of America's School Leaders and High School Students."

[12] Brenda J. Turnbull, M. Bruce Haslam, Erikson R. Arcaira, Derek L. Riley, Beth Sinclair, Stephen Coleman, *Evaluation of the School Administration Manager Project* (Washington, DC: Policy Study Associates, 2009), iii–iv.

[13] Turnbull et al., *Evaluation of the School Administration Manager Project*, 42–43.

[14]Kristina Smekens now has a business that provides this kind of professional development for teachers on issues related to writing, reading, and comprehension. She has trained staff members who provide live workshops, school consulting, and remote coaching.

[15]Many principals would reject a 60-hour work week as incompatible with work-life balance. I was able to put in this many hours because of my position in the life cycle. I didn't have small children at home anymore and both my husband and I were focused on developing our respective careers. I was committed to doing whatever I could to implement my two-rules philosophy to help the students at Fall Ridge.

[16]Jason A. Grissom, Anna J. Egalite, and Constance A. Lindsay, *How Principals Affect Students and Schools: A Systematic Synthesis of Two Decades of Research* (New York: The Wallace Foundation, 2021), 54, http://www.wallace-foundation.org/principalsynthesis.

[17]Grissom, et al., *How Principals Affect Students and Schools*, 56.

[18]Grissom, et al., *How Principals Affect Students and Schools*, 57.

[19]Richard Elmore, *Building a New Structure for School Leadership* (Albert Shanker Institute, 2000), 15, https://files.eric.ed.gov/fulltext/ED546618.pdf.

[20]Alma Harris, "Distributed Leadership: According to the Evidence," *Journal of Educational Administration*, 46, no. 2 (2008): 172–188.

[21]Sullivan, "Principals Are on the Brink of a Breakdown."

[22]Elizabeth D. Steiner, Sy Doan, Ashley Woo, Allyson D. Gittens, Rebecca Ann Lawrence, Lisa Berdie, Rebecca L. Wolfe, Lucas Greer, and Heather L. Schwartz, "Restoring Teacher and Principal Well-Being Is an Essential Step for Rebuilding Schools: Findings from the State of the American Teacher and State of the American Principal Surveys," Rand Corporation, 2022, 13, https://www.rand.org/pubs/research_reports/RRA1108-4.html.

[23]Steiner et al., "Restoring Teacher and Principal Well-Being Is an Essential Step," 15.

[24]The NASSP's 2022 survey found that 38 percent of principals were planning to leave "their current role" within three years. "NASSP's Survey of America's School Leaders and High School Students."

[25]"NASSP's Survey of America's School Leaders and High School Students," n.d. (2022 data), https://survey.nassp.org/2022/#intro.

[26]"NASSP Survey Signals a Looming Mass Exodus of Principals from Schools," news release, December 8, 2021, https://www.nassp.org/news/nassp-survey-signals-a-looming-mass-exodus-of-principals-from-schools/.

[27]Steiner et al., "Restoring Teacher and Principal Well-Being Is an Essential Step," 19.

[28]Meg Stomski, Xueqin Lin, Hua Luo, Dr. Rebecca Cheung, and Dr. Chunyan Yang, "Finding Resilience during the COVID-19 Pandemic: Perspectives from School Leaders," 21CSLA Project Brief 1, no. 1 (March 2022): 5, 2, https://drive.google.com/file/d/12Oc9h6lV_TJqq-ICdHpQDwWDOsCRNtrP/view.

[29]Stomski et al., "Finding Resilience during the COVID-19 Pandemic."

[30]"21CSLA Research-Practice Webinar: Principal Resilience (May 19, 2022)," https://21cslacenter.berkeley.edu/file/202.

[31]Santos Gonzalez, in "21CSLA Research-Practice Webinar: Principal Resilience," at 50:40.

[32]Rebecca Cheung, executive director, UCB Leadership Programs and leadership coach with 21CSLA, in "21CSLA Research-Practice Webinar: Principal Resilience," at 48:33.

[33]Meg Stomski, Xueqin Lin, Hua Luo, Aukeem A. Ballard, Dr. Rebecca Cheung, and Dr. Chunyan Yang, "Finding Resilience during the COVID-19 Pandemic: Perspectives from School Leaders," 21CSLA Project Brief 1, no. 2 (September 2022): 6.

[34]Shane Safir, "Six Ways to Support and Sustain Quality Principals," NASSP, November 2019, https://www.nassp.org/publication/principal-leadership/volume-20/principal-leadership-november-2019/principal-well-being-a-missing-link/.

About the Author

Brenda's remarkable journey began in Georgetown, Illinois, where she grew up as the youngest of the family. She has an older sister and brother born in Campbellsville, Kentucky. The family relocated to Illinois as her father followed the pipeline to find better work and took a job at the General Motors Plant in Danville, Illinois.

Despite her parents lacking the privilege of formal education, they instilled in Brenda the profound importance of learning, laying the foundation for her extraordinary educational journey.

Her upbringing gave her the determination to break new ground in her family. Brenda blazed a trail as the first to embark on the path of higher education. Immediately following her high school graduation, she eagerly enrolled in undergraduate studies coursework at Danville Area Community College. Her parents wanted her to graduate from college before they would approve of her marriage. She graduated with an Associate in Applied Science degree from Danville Area Community College.

After graduating, Brenda and her high school sweetheart, Zeke, forged a life together, beginning with their shared journey in the United States Navy. They moved to different locations, but their true happiness lay in the blessings of family life. They cherish their beautiful daughter, Sarah, who, inspired by her mother's footsteps, became a special education teacher. The family expanded further with the addition of a wonderful son-in-law, Alex, and the arrival of precious grandchildren—Aubrey, Abram, and Alden.

Brenda's professional journey in the education field was diverse and deeply fulfilling. Her career commenced as a teaching assistant, where she shared her knowledge and passion with eager young minds. Over the years, she embraced various roles, including serving as a dedicated Technology Teacher for grades K–5, a nurturing fifth-grade classroom teacher, and rising to assume leadership positions as Assistant Principal, Elementary Principal, and Middle School Principal. Her unwavering commitment to education and her students was a constant throughout her journey. Her dedication culminated in her elevation to the district-level role of Director of Educational Support Programs, where she continued to influence the education landscape.

Brenda's impact extended far beyond the school doors. She emerged as a dedicated community leader, actively participating in multiple community boards and generously contributing her expertise and generosity to various local initiatives. Her commitment was equally fervent within the Illinois Principal Association, where she served in multiple capacities, including Illini Regional Director, Professional Development Provider, and Administrator Academy Provider. She represented her peers on various state committees and even served as the Treasurer of the Illinois Association of Title Directors, later being elected Vice President. Brenda's passion for service remained unwavering as she continued to pay it forward, serving as a coach and mentor for principals and aspiring principals, guiding them on their journeys of leadership and service.

Throughout her life, Brenda's profound passion was evident in her unyielding commitment to serving others. Whether providing resources, offering solutions, or simply extending a supportive hand, Brenda's influence was felt in communities far and wide. Her life story is a testament to the power of determination, resilience, education, and an indomitable desire to provide solutions every day.

Brenda's life has been marked by extraordinary challenges, including battles with Crohn's Disease, surviving a lightning strike, overcoming breast cancer, and enduring a near-fatal car crash, which left her with life-changing injuries. Despite these hardships, Brenda views them as lessons and blessings, fortifying her spirit. She believes that every day is an opportunity to make a choice. She encourages others to be the authors of their own stories, making choices that shape their paths. Brenda firmly believes that we have the power to react, respond, reflect, and review how we think, speak, and act, thereby shaping the narrative of our lives.

Connect with her by following her on LinkedIn, X (formerly Twitter), Instagram, and her website, brendayoho.com. She has some sayings she is known for: "Be the solution daily." "Education is something we do with children, not to them." "You can choose to be part of the problem or the solution; the choice is always yours."

www.ingramcontent.com/pod-product-compliance
Lightning Source LLC
Chambersburg PA
CBHW070750160726
48004CB00001B/132